BETWEEN THE
SEXES

—————— LISA SOWLE CAHILL ——————

BETWEEN THE SEXES

Foundations for a Christian Ethics of Sexuality

FORTRESS PRESS
Philadelphia

COPYRIGHT © 1985 BY FORTRESS PRESS

Library of Congress Cataloging in Publication Data

Cahill, Lisa Sowle.
  Between the sexes.

  Based on the 1983 E.T. Earl lectures at the Pacific
School of Religion, Berkeley, Calif.
  Bibliography: p.
  Includes index.
  1. Sex—Religious aspects—Christianity—Addresses,
essays, lectures.   2. Christian ethics—Addresses,
essays, lectures.   I. Title.
BT708.C28   1985   241'.66   84-48717
ISBN 0-8006-1834-3

Printed in the United States of America   1—1834
94   93   92   5   6   7   8   9   10

To my two good friends,
James M. Gustafson
and
Lawrence R. Cahill

ACKNOWLEDGMENTS

The chapters to follow began as the 1983 E. T. Earl Lectures at the Pacific School of Religion, Berkeley, California. Had the president of the Pacific School of Religion, Neely D. McCarter, not honored me with an invitation to become the eighty-second lecturer in the series (and had he not specified my topic), I might never have had the temerity to engage at such length so puzzling and provocative a subject as Christian ethics of sexuality. The scholars, pastors, and other thoughtful Christians who responded both formally and informally to my six lectures encouraged me to continue the work begun, and with helpful criticism pressed me toward reexamination of presuppositions and refinement of arguments. The final product is much better for it.

I mention my teacher and friend James M. Gustafson in the dedication of this book because, despite its inevitable shortcomings, I trust it to exemplify at least the respect for clearsightedness, balance, and appreciation of truths within divergent convictions that Jim inspires in all his students. In particular, he taught me and other Roman Catholics who shared his Wednesday afternoon seminars at the University of Chicago Divinity School to suspect that even a good Thomist might profitably read the Bible and come to contemplate whether the challenges it presents to the natural law theologian and the moral philosopher are significant.

I also am indebted to my husband, Larry. It is not always easy to be wedded to an academic, and not always comfortable to reply to friendly inquiries that one's wife is writing a book about sex. For their support in trying circumstances of many sorts, I thank all my family, especially Larry.

Collegial consultation in writing this book has been especially important because of its interdisciplinary character. Biblical scholars at Boston College have been patient as well as generous in the face of my continual impositions on their time, talents, and libraries. It is Pheme Perkins who most frequently has saved me from the amateur's blunders, but my nuisance value for Cheryl Exum, Anthony J. Saldarini, and Susan Praeder also has been high. One of the first to stimulate my interest in taking marriage seriously as a matter for theological attention was Theodore Mackin, S.J., with whom I studied as an undergraduate at Santa Clara, but who has continued to educate me with his writings about marriage in the Catholic Church.

As when any beleaguered academic gives birth to a book, there are many others who have cooperated in midwifery: administrators at Boston College, especially William B. Neenan, S.J., Dean of Arts and Sciences, who facilitated financial support in the preparation of the manuscript; the Theology Department staff (especially Mary E. Robinson and Lisa Foley), who coordinated typing and corrections of drafts; my research assistant, Douglas Clark, who shared the task of indexing; my editor at Fortress Press, John A. Hollar, who demanded that I translate "academese" into intelligible English; and finally but most importantly, the other women, Sarah Zopf Bent and Ruth (Doo Young) Lee, who helped love and care for my children while I was at the office writing about marriage and parenthood, and in doing so, allowed me to maximize the time in which I could enjoy being with Charlotte and James, learning from them things one does not learn in books.

CONTENTS

— 1 —

SEXUALITY
AND CHRISTIAN ETHICS:
How to Proceed

This book is about two subjects. It is about the "rights and wrongs" of relationship between women and men, and it is about how to make a good argument. At a fundamental level, it is about the riskiness and promise of discovering just what makes Christian ethics Christian, and what constitutes a convincing case about right and wrong from a Christian point of view; and at the level of application, it is about sexual ethics and the ethics of male and female cooperation.

Both sexual ethics and ethical methodology clearly are problems, which is what makes their discussion not only interesting but urgent. One of the many reasons sex is of interest for every adult human being is that all people at least some of the time are unsure how to understand their sexuality and how to behave sexually in ways that are morally praiseworthy rather than reprehensible. Moreover, ethicists want to talk theoretically and normatively about sexuality and sex in ways that are not only praiseworthy but coherent. This ambition too is problematic, peculiarly so for the Christian ethicist. He or she has to take into account factors and perspectives that seem to lead in opposed directions. These include common wisdom; what the empirical studies, which presently command so much attention, reveal about human sexual experience and gender identity; the ways Christian authors and churches traditionally have educated the faithful to perceive male and female relations, sexuality, and sex; what the Bible says or indicates about these subjects; and even central philosophical presentations of them. Perhaps the salient obligation

1

of the moral analyst, given this state of affairs, is to muster the nerve to proceed at all.

Despite its pitfalls, the task of analysis may not be avoided. For humans, "sexuality" is "morality." It is part of our expressing, for good or ill, relationship to the material world, to other life forms, to the self, and to other persons, including God. As our point of departure we will pay attention to the experiential phenomena of sex and sexuality, for they bring home in a most pressing and universal manner the necessity of systematic reflection on the moral life.

SEXUAL EXPERIENCE

Sex is now no more a simple matter than it ever has been, however much in the name of "sexual liberation" we claim to have demystified it. Twentieth-century Americans are no more or less obsessed with sex than our predecessors; it is only that our obsessions take different forms. Sex, despite its prosaic side, was to our grandparents' generation a hidden idol, enshrined in an aura of mystery, fascination, and danger; we glorify, pursue, and parade it to the point of banality. Sex has been connected with elemental and divine powers in certain historical periods and cultures; but our protestations that it is "natural" do not conceal our own fear and even contempt of it. Why is it that sex among human beings is always so puzzling? Why are humans not able, like other animals, to come together by instinctual motives of self- and species preservation, to couple briefly, to conceive, and thereafter to part or affiliate (without problems), motivated again by instinct to do what is necessary to raise the young that result?

It seems to be precisely the animal-like compulsion of sexual yearning that most bewilders and beleaguers the human moral agent, philosopher, and theologian. Augustine of Hippo referred to "the shameful motion of the organs of generation"[1] and went so far as to suggest that in the Garden of Eden sexual intercourse between Adam and Eve would have taken place without any sexual desire at all. Apparently, it seemed to Augustine that the replacement of disorderly passion by a sheer act of the rational will would have been more in keeping with human dignity.[2] While this theory may be extreme, it does represent an influential Christian author's perception of the ambivalence of human sexual experience.[3] Humans have tended to conclude from reflection on the matter that sexual impulses either are in an essential sense anti-human because they cannot be conformed to some ideal of pure rationality and freedom, of absolute self-control; or, on the other side, are so quintessentially, immediately, and irresistibly natural that it is as futile to deny, suppress, or sublimate them as it would be the contractions of the heart muscle. Human beings have a preference for thinking in extremes; it makes matters far more simple. But simplicity in human affairs is more often than not illusory. Sexuality is no exception. Some accounts of human sexuality and its genital expressions construe them as counter-human because they are among those experiences in which humans feel least in control of themselves and most under the influence of instincts and physical responses. To the minds of some of the fathers of the Christian tradition, sexual desire is to be resisted lest it bring humanity to the level of the animals. Such interpretations miss the obvious point that "animality" is not a pejorative term and that, indeed, it is one aptly applied to the species Homo sapiens.[4] But accounts of sex that explain it as a simple, universal, and irresistibly attractive drive ignore the fact that humans are animals of a special sort. Their ability to reflect self-consciously and empathetically on their own and others' needs and interests, to discriminate cognitively and affectively among them in terms of immediate and long-range outcomes, and to act so as to rearrange priorities and redirect impulses in the interests of communities and of other persons is not unparalleled in the animal world, but it is nowhere matched.

We have, then, a certain duality in sexual experience. It is physical, urgent, and pervasive. It is also an avenue of affective and spiritual relations among persons, for good or ill. Yet the human person is not a duality. At least Western philosophical and religious traditions have learned to resist dualistic interpretations of the person, even if they have not overcome them. To cut the person into separate pieces of soul and body, psyche and physique, freedom and determinacy, is again too simple. We shall note that the Genesis creation accounts attest that the human being is one, a unity, which has two aspects but not two discrete components.

It is this duality of experience in unity of being that grounds the problem of human sexuality. Sex in humans is not understood completely if it is explained only as a physiologic species-survival mechanism, or a technique of physical enjoyment. It is also an instrument, or indeed a constituent, of the sorts of interpersonal relations that are most distinctively human. Since humans are as capable of evil, wickedness, selfishness, and manipulation in these relationships as they are of good, rectitude, self-sacrifice, and generosity, sex is a problem. And sinfulness in sex, as in other realms of human existence, often springs from just the fact that humans are slothful and cowardly and shortsighted, and thus refuse to take on the project of reconciling the troublesome human reality of what Reinhold Niebuhr called freedom and finitude, or spirit and nature.[5] The ever-mobile, dialectical relation between these poles is what makes the human situation so precarious and causes our anxiety. It is because we cannot resolve this anxiety, and refuse to endure it, that we attempt to evade it. In so doing, according to Niebuhr, we sin by denial of what it is to be human.

I fear that this beginning has had about it an air of moroseness which, I hope, does not represent adequately the sexual experiences of most people, even of most Christians. But I see it as the necessary backdrop for the project of ascertaining what the Christian religious tradition demands of humans in their sexual being and relationships and acts. It is this ambiguous, problematic quality of sex that has instigated much of the worrying and writing about it that has gone on in Christianity. No doubt, in a profound way sexuality will remain an enigma. It would be naive, ahistorical, and self-aggrandizing to think that we might achieve an unassailable or even unique formulation of the problem of sexuality and its ethical resolution. But we may come to understand it more adequately, if never completely, by recollecting and critically renewing what some of our predecessors have had to say of our common experience.

THE SOURCES OF
CHRISTIAN ETHICS

But what are the wellsprings of this process? The interrelation and priority of the sources of Christian ethics is the major methodological theme of these chapters. This concern is another version of the "reason and revelation" question. How ought the Christian ethicist to include, interpret, and weigh religious and secular sources of moral insight? Not infrequently, Christian authors writing about sexual ethics so stress a chosen point of departure that the contributions of other sources are neglected or virtually excluded. Whether one begins with, for instance, received "natural law" teaching, certain biblical prohibitions, or scientific studies of sexual psychology and behavior, a fully "Christian" process of reflection will permit interpretation and qualification of that initial source by other complementary ones.[6] My thesis, whose lack of originality may be its strength, is that there are four complementary reference points for Christian ethics:[7] the foundational texts or "scriptures" of the faith community—the Bible; the community's "tradition" of faith, theology, and practice; philosophical accounts of essential or ideal humanity ("normative" accounts of the human[8]); and descriptions of what actually is and has been the case in human lives and societies ("descriptive" accounts of the human). While Scripture is the reference point most obviously associated with Christian theological ethics, empirical sciences recently have received most emphasis as sources of insight into human sexuality, sexual behavior, marriage, parenthood, and gender roles. Both Bible and empirical studies present particular problems for the ethicist, for they entail special, internal canons of interpretation, with which the theological ethicist may not have sophisticated familiarity. Yet both sources are indispensable for contemporary Christian ethics. Sometimes Christian theologians have rejected the adequacy for a Christian moral perspective of nonreligious definitions of the normatively human ("human nature"), but Christian ethics is never uninfluenced by secular philosophical anthropologies, even those against which it defines itself. Because it is the fundamental content for explicitly theological ethical reflection, the Christian tradition forms the "hermeneutical circle" within which Christian theology defines itself and interprets its other sources. The most distinctive source of Christian ethics, the Bible, is the product of the most primitive stage in the life history of the community founded in Christ. In a sense, the Bible is not only the basis of the Christian religious tradition, but is actually a representation of the first phases within that tradition. Although "tradition" is sometimes taken to mean dogmatic or moral propositions transmitted from the past, it is better understood as the "story" of a people, "handed on" or "transmitted" for reappropriation in each generation. It includes but is not limited to formulations of dogma and ethics derived from the faith life of the community. Specific criteria for what counts as "tradition" might include antiquity, widespread usage, consensus of the faithful, and authoritative definition. Tradition is the historical identity and self-understanding of the religious community, which is formed by the Scriptures, and which continues to inform its present and future.[9]

I contend that fidelity to these four mutually correcting sources, and success in judiciously balancing them, is a standard by which we can measure the adequacy of various positions in the tradition, including our own. Thomas Aquinas, for example, gives priority to the philosophical element in ethics. He interprets the relation of man and woman, marriage, and procreation on the basis of his understanding of what it would mean to be fully and authentically human, that is, to live in accord with the nature that God bestows in the creation. His philosophical anthropology, however, is informed in a radical way not only by that of Aristotle but also by the perspective of medieval Christianity. Although Thomas accomplishes much in terms of a reasonable account of human existence, he neglects a primary source to which Martin Luther redirects our attention: the Bible. With his radical insistence that ethics be ordered by Scripture, and *sola Scriptura*, Luther revitalizes the nature of Christian ethics as the delineation of the practical consequences of faith and life in Christ. In filling out the details and ramifications of the biblical witness for sexuality and marriage, however, Luther relies a great deal on common experience and common sense. Even the inspired Word of God in Scripture is not a sheer "datum" but an occasion of hearing and understanding the spirit of the Lord present in community.

In contemporary theology, the realization is increasing that it is no easy matter to determine how these four resources of Bible, tradition, and descriptive and normative accounts of the human should be balanced. This is especially so, given the facts that no one source is understood apart from the complementary contributions of the others; and that their perspectives on some moral issues may in the end diverge. Chapter 8, which concerns the evaluation of some specific types of sexual relations, furnishes the occasion for a confrontation of the question whether the four may in some instances be incompatible. For example, the Bible seems to provide clearly negative evaluations of homosexual behavior. Empirical and quantitative studies, however, offer evidence that homosexuality is a result of nature or environment, not choice, that it occurs cross-culturally, and that even an overt homosexual lifestyle of itself precludes neither psychological and social health, nor the exercise of central virtues traditionally associated with Christ-like living. We will also have occasion to examine the interface of biblical and empirical studies when we take up the problem of male and female sex differences and gender roles. On either of these questions, homosexuality or gender roles, the ethicist's commitment to his or her task is complicated by the awareness that even the collection of so-called "objective empirical data" is made possible by categories of organization which are not without interpretative elements. By what "scientific" standard, for example, is one's sexual orientation defined as "homosexual" or "heterosexual"; or is a person of either orientation described as "socially well-adjusted"? Or, what are the presuppositions that determine the patterns of family organization that the anthropologist chooses to study? On what premises does he or she draw lines of causation between adult female and male roles in a given society, and that society's patterns of child rearing, or religious symbols, or economic and political systems? What we look for and eventually see in what "is" cannot but be influenced, if not determined, by what we think "ought to be." The ethicist who uses or rejects empirical studies naively will pay with loss of credibility, not only to the broader culture or to the "academy" but also to those in the church who perceive that Christian existence is a form of human experience.[10]

The interpretative problem with which I am most concerned is that of a critical hermeneutic of the Christian Scriptures which is cognizant both of historical-critical research on the biblical texts and their communities of authorship and of the authoritative character of the Scriptures for the ongoing life of the community of faith. Chapter 2 involves an extended discussion of biblical hermeneutics, an area fundamental to Christian ethics and one in which fascinating and important controversies are today being waged.

TOWARD A CHRISTIAN ETHICS
OF SEXUALITY

The most important biblical contribution to a Christian ethics of sexual activity and of relationship between the sexes is the placement of morality within the life of the faith community. Morality is not an interest for its own sake, but for the sake of understanding how the people of God will live and act toward one another and toward others if they are faithful. In the Hebrew Bible or Christian Old Testament, the covenant with Yahweh leads to certain religious and moral forms of existence which are an expression of covenant fidelity. In the New Testament, faith and conversion in Jesus Christ establish membership in the Spirit-filled community. The Christian bears the "fruits of the Spirit," or certain qualities of character that dispose one to act in certain ways. Sexuality receives some attention as a concrete mode of action, but certainly far less than we are inclined to give it.

In examining the biblical witness for sexual morality, we will focus on patterns of male-female relationship and sexual relations that can be referred broadly to canonical material, rather than on the specific content of isolated texts.

Both Old and New Testament resources support a view of sexuality as part of the goodness of humanity's creation, but as also subject to the corruption of sin. Humanity is essentially male and female. Man and woman are created for a physical, procreative, psychological, and social partnership, which presupposes sexual differentiation but not hierarchy. Human sexual acts fulfill cooperation and express community, but are in themselves never the focus of biblical discussions. Morality for both the Hebrew and Christian communities is one aspect of cohesive living in obedience and fidelity. While I would judge that the biblical literature points toward heterosexual, monogamous, lifelong, and procreative marriage as the normative or ideal institutionalization of sexual activity, I would not say that the biblical texts represent preoccupation with, or indeed much interest in, the justification or exclusion of other sexual expressions. It will be necessary to turn to additional resources of Christian ethics both to confirm the general scriptural views of male and female, of human sexuality, and of sexual acts; and to consider in what ways the scriptural norm can be realized or adapted in variable concrete situations. As the New Testament divorce texts show us, the process of adaptation begins already within the canon.

Christian authors do better or worse in developing a theology of human sexuality in proportion to their ability to consider, relate, and balance these sources. When the influence of one or more is ignored or minimized, the position becomes less secure. We have indicated already that Thomas Aquinas respects a philosophical perspective on human sexuality, but is not very critical of his cultural milieu and largely neglects the Bible. Luther uses the Bible to criticize received tradition, but finds it necessary to interpret the Bible in the light of concrete experience.

We too will need to complement our reading of the Bible and to respond to the mores of our own culture by attending to all the reference points of Christian ethics. Of the Christian tradition it will be asked what the community of faith consistently has affirmed about human sexuality. A response might suggest the goodness of sexuality as God's creation, male and female differentiation and union, the importance of procreation as a purpose of sexual acts, marriage and family as the institutionalization of procreation, and the social partnership of male and female. The tradition, however, also yields elements that today are regarded as less than normative: the dubious moral nature of all sex, the subordination of women, and intended procreation as the only complete justification of sexual acts. The ambiguity of the tradition, as well as of the Bible, presses us to the question of *criteria* for the elimination or appropriation of biblical and traditional meanings of sexuality and sexual activity. The standard of an adequate Christian theology and ethics of sexuality is precisely the dialectical and complementary relationship of Bible, tradition, and normative and descriptive accounts of human existence.

Since moral philosophy and philosophical anthropologies have many incarnations, it is difficult to isolate a single normative view of the human as central. In chapter 6, Thomas Aquinas will exemplify one central view of human nature. The classical, medieval, and modern world views entail different presuppositions about whether what is "natural" to humans can be known in any clear and final way, and about whether human "nature" may indeed change. But philosophical accounts of sexual ethics commonly presuppose that it is possible to define at least approximately some "essential" or "ideal" meaning of sexuality, despite actual historical distortions or adaptations of it in the human sexual reality, and despite the limits of the human mind seeking to discover it. Sometimes, of course, such definitions are used in the service of a religious tradition or culture and its view of sexuality, and thus transmit some of the same "values" that were defined above as inadequate components of the Christian tradition. However, most moral philosophers today, as well as some classical ones, at least to a degree, may be understood to affirm the essential character of sex in relation to human being, the meaning of sex as expression of interpersonal relation as well as procreation, and the equal dignity of man and woman.

Descriptive accounts of what the human situation actually is like gives us a "window" onto the normative. In our century, the empirical sciences have become preeminent sources of such factual information. Another form of describing the human situation is the "personal story," which is then generalized, implicitly or explicitly, to persons in situations similar to that of the author of the account. Empirical or other descriptive resources serve as correctives to biblical, traditional, and normative accounts that simply do not correspond to the realities of human experience. Although it is a departure from what could be thought of as a natural progression from Bible to tradition to modern ethical reflection, I have included an analysis of gender roles (chapter 5) in the light of recent empirical studies after my discussion of biblical views of male and female, and before that of two representatives of Christian tradition, Aquinas and Luther. The reasons for the order are three. First, it will encourage appreciation of the fact that "the Bible" is not some point of departure in the past but the continuing platform of response to accompanying sources of moral insight, which, in turn, enable more adequate appropriation of the Bible itself as a norm. Second, a better perspective on the ways Thomas Aquinas and Martin Luther arrive at and use presuppositions about what "really" is the case in human experience will be facilitated by a contrast of their methods of investigation with more directly quantitative and empirical ones. Finally, by breaking any impression of a neat, ostensibly historical progression through the four sources, I hope to demonstrate in practice what I propose in theory: that the relation between the sources of Christian ethics is ever dialectical, circular, and critical.

Finally, in chapter 8, I will draw together my reflections on Bible, tradition, philosophy, and scientific studies in order to offer some normative suggestions for a Christian ethics of sexual activity. To put it briefly, I will offer that the Christian community has in the past evaluated and should continue to evaluate sexual expression by the two criteria of commitment and procreative responsibility. Particular sexual acts and relations can realize these values in different ways and in different degrees, however. Not all traditionally "Christian" interpretations of these criteria should continue to determine moral analysis of sexuality.

Although I hope to show that attention to several sources will be profitable for Christian ethics, especially a Christian ethics of sexuality, I must acknowledge at the outset that my proposals, both methodological and substantive, will be provisional. For one, the quadruple enumeration of Christian ethics' sources certainly will be subject to restatement or refinement. For another, assessment of their contributions can be carried out most successfully by those who have in regard to them more specialized expertise than I. By no means have I discussed Bible, tradition, philosophy, and descriptions of actual experience comprehensively. I have chosen instead to focus on certain aspects of each, with the aim of demonstrating the interconnection of our understanding of any one with that of all the others. My purpose in writing will have been accomplished if others are induced to undertake more proficiently the task, which I have set for myself, of construing Christian ethics as a dynamic yet ordered form of fidelity to the central Christian symbols of beneficent Creator, righteous Judge, gracious Redeemer, and transforming Spirit. These symbols require us to attend to our own experience, to view critically all our ideas and actions, and to take the experience of God in community as the beginning point of reconciliation of body and spirit, self and others, and humanity and God.

NOTES

1. Augustine, *City of God* XIV. 19, 21.

2. Ibid., XIV. 23–24.

3. Although the "irresistibility" of sexual drives indeed has been a major component in Christian reflection on sexual ethics, I wonder if it is not more an element of the male experience of sex than of the female. It was precisely the involuntary movements of the male sexual organ that Augustine seemed to find so shameful and even frightening. (See David F. Kelly, "Sexuality and Concupiscence in Augustine," in *The Annual of the Society of Christian Ethics: 1983*, ed. Larry L. Rasmussen [Southern Methodist University: Society of Christian Ethics, 1983].) A complementary (not opposite) female perspective on the experience of sexuality was offered by Karen Lebacqz, who was a member of a panel that responded to my Earl Lectures at the Pacific School of Religion (February 1983). Lebacqz offered that our sexuality is an avenue of *vulnerability*, because through it we both need and are open to other persons. Lebacqz did not suggest that vulnerability is a characteristic of the woman's sexuality only, nor is the experience of an urgent physical drive only the man's. However, the male and female experiences of sexuality (which certainly differ physically and may differ psychologically and emotionally) may enable men and women to be more sensitive to its various aspects. The philosopher Sara Ruddick also comments that in the most complete sexual exchanges "vulnerability is increased for *both* sexes by the active desiring of the partners" ("Better Sex," in *Philosophy and Sex*, ed. Robert Baker and Frederick Elliston [Buffalo: Prometheus Books, 1975], 97).

4. Mary Midgley, *Beast and Man* (Ithaca, N.Y.: Cornell Univ. Press, 1978).

5. Reinhold Niebuhr, *The Nature and Destiny of Man*, vol. 1 (New York: Charles Scribner's Sons, 1964), chap. 7.

6. For a critical discussion of the use of sources in recent Christian ethics of sexuality, see my "Sexual Issues in Christian Theological Ethics: A Review of Recent Studies," *Religious Studies Review* 4/1 (1978): 1–14.

7. Several who heard the Earl Lectures pointed out the resemblance of my method to the Methodist "quadrilateral" test, inspired by John Wesley. Although this test is formulated somewhat differently, I take its similarity to confirm my conviction that the sources I name are no novelty, but substantive for Christian theology and ethics. Another discussion of the method of Christian ethics, which resembles mine in appealing to several sources but which is much more exhaustive, is provided by Robert J. Daly, *Christian Biblical Ethics: From Biblical Revelation to Contemporary Christian Praxis* (New York: Paulist Press, 1984). See especially Part 1, chap. 3, "The Bible and Ethics." The book began in a task force of the Catholic Biblical Association, and incorporates chapters by members of that group, woven by Daly into a lengthy study. Daly and others raise many of the hermeneutical questions that I do, come to a consensus that Christian ethics is both a science and an art, and address issues of practice such as nonviolence, marriage, divorce, and politics.

8. "The normatively human" is a phrase borrowed from James M. Gustafson ("Genetic Engineering and a Normative View of the Human," in *Ethical Issues in Biology and Medicine*, ed. Preston N. Williams [Cambridge: Schenkman, 1972], 46–58). It indicates what is to be valued and promoted in human existence, or what is fulfilling for humanity, but is free of the connotation of the classical term "human nature" that essential human being is an ahistorical and clearly knowable entity.

9. See James Hennesey, S.J., "Grasping the Tradition: Reflections of a Church Historian," *Theological Studies* 45/1 (1984): 153–63.

10. In chap. 1 of *The Analogical Imagination: Christian Theology and the Culture of Pluralism* (New York: Crossroad, 1981), David Tracy speaks of the three "publics" of theology: society, academy, and church (pp. 3–46).

— 2 —

THE BIBLE
AND ETHICS:
Hermeneutical
Dilemmas

The Christian community by definition takes the Bible as a source, even the primary source, of its identity. But ever since the emergence of historical-critical methods of investigating biblical materials and communities of authorship, the claim that the Bible has authority for faith and theology has taken new shapes.[1] One reason is that historical studies have revealed the particular social and cultural concerns shaping theological positions in the Bible. Another is that these studies have heightened awareness that those positions are quite diverse. As the products of very different religious communities, they prove difficult to unify around a common theme or concept. As a result, the project of discovering a cohesive "theology of the Bible" or "biblical theology" has become dubious.

In recent years the nature of biblical authority has been redefined with the help of three guiding questions. First, what is the significance of biblical diversity? Is the biblical collection as a whole or "canon" in any sense authoritative? The New Testament scholar James Dunn has inquired with a note of dismay, "Did the earliest Christians hold *nothing* in common?"[2] The theologian—or ethicist— suspects with some trepidation that he may be right in his claim that what the canon "canonizes" is "the diversity of Christianity"![3] Furthermore, if diversity is a problem, it is not the only one. There is also the difficulty of getting *from* a meaning or coherence of meanings *to* the situation of a later religious community with its own, perhaps different, concerns. A second question results: How can Scripture be used as a norm for particular doctrinal or ethical judg-

15

ments, as well as for general theological perspectives? If Scripture is the "authority" just how does it provide specific "authorizations" capable of settling controverted issues?[4] One way to deal both with the problem of multiplicity and with that of cultural conditioning would be to bring to the Bible some external criterion or criteria by which to distinguish more and less authoritative, or nonauthoritative, elements. This leads to our third question: is Scripture *alone* authoritative, or is its normativity modified by the contributions of other sources? To put it another way, to what extent does the identity of Christians converge with that of those who do not share Christianity's distinctive narratives, images, and ideals? Do their sources of self-understanding coincide, and what is the import of this?

In contemporary biblical scholarship these questions are approached with an appreciation of the vital importance of the historicity of the religious traditions that produced the biblical literature, of its authors, of the final or "canonical" expressions of those traditions, and of later communities of interpretation. The "norm of Scripture" is not accessible in any "pure," unambiguous form since we neither receive nor interpret it in an ahistorical, acultural, and value-free vacuum. The fact that the Scriptures are the voices of historical communities of faith which command the hearing of ongoing communities shaped by and shaping those Scriptures' authority has important implications. First, it means that the very definition of "Scripture" as an "authoritative" collection depends on the existence and contribution of a "tradition" that so regards it. This entails that its authority also depends indirectly on the other sources of self-understanding of the persons and communities who constitute that tradition. Some of these sources will be nonreligious. Second, it explains why there may be no "unified" view of an issue in the canon and why it is impossible to use the whole canon as a resource for a particular moral "authorization." Finally, it means that such "authorizations" or warrants for moral conclusions will be formulated, proposed, and evaluated in a complex historical, cultural, and religious context which will influence the process of authorization itself.

HISTORICAL CRITICISM,
BIBLICAL DIVERSITY,
AND CANON

As we have seen, to ask the question whether the biblical literature enjoys authority uniformly is to raise the issue of what it means to speak of an authoritative "canon." Put simply, the canon is that body of written materials that the believing community has in practice and over a period of time come to accept as definitive of its faith. A more refined definition would address the criteria for a process of canonization; the distinguishing marks of canonical books, as versus noncanonical ones, if any common marks are discernible; the senses in which the canon might be said to be "revealed," "inspired," or "inerrant";[5] and whether and why the canon is or is not definitively closed.[6] The significant point for ethics is that traditionally the whole canon in sum and parts has been taken in principle to be authoritative, even though in practice its interpreters have been partial to passages or books congenial to their viewpoints. On the whole, theologians have operated with a presumption in favor of the ultimate integrity of the canon and of the compatibility of religious, moral, and theological perspectives therein represented. That biblical scholarship has undercut any naive form of this presumption is hardly in question today.

By showing that the *Sitz im Leben* or "life setting" of a biblical text in Israelite history or in primitive Christianity is formative of and reflected in the text's final shape, modern historical criticism cemented the post-Enlightenment realization that biblical portraits of God and Jesus reflect diverse religious and theological agendas and thus are themselves multiple in meaning. Twenty years ago, Ernst Käsemann radically called into question the supposition that biblical authors are treating different but complementary aspects of one central tradition by insisting that theological positions within the New Testament sometimes are articulated in *opposition* to one another. From this he concluded that any normative conclusions from the Bible for Christian theology must be premised on a selective reading which disallows the authority of some religious images or theological models while preferring others.[7]

The Christian ethicist can appreciate the merit of this claim. He or she will not have been slow to notice that, beyond intracanonical diversity, there exist in the Bible moral prescriptions, and especially prohibitions, which seem in the light of more recent reflection to be not merely dispensable but wrong. And this is true not only of specific moral rules but also of some general moral standpoints represented within the canonical literature. Examples having to do with sexuality and gender roles are plentiful both in Israelite law (e.g., Leviticus), and the epistles of Paul and the Pastorals. For example, anyone who commits a homosexual act is denounced as categorically cut off from God (Lev. 18:22; 20:13; Rom. 24:27), adultery is categorized as a capital crime (Lev. 20:10), and women are enjoined to accept male domination as God's will (1 Tim. 2:8–15). Some have concluded that the fact that such biblical teachings are historically conditioned means that their authority is radically relative to their original settings. Elisabeth Schüssler Fiorenza, in attempting a feminist reconstruction and interpretation of the New Testament witness, insists not only that "biblical texts are not verbally inspired revelation nor doctrinal principles but historical formulations within the context of a religious community," but also that "all texts are products of an androcentric patriarchal culture and history."[8]

If diverse biblical witnesses cannot be reconciled, or even brought into a pattern of mutual toleration, then is the conclusion unavoidable that only some parts are normative? If so, are there any uniform, persuasive criteria for distinguishing such parts? Is our selection of privileged texts and themes arbitrary or itself relative to biases furnished by our own culture? These questions will be especially pressing in regard to the ambiguous significance of the Pauline, deutero-Pauline, and pastoral epistles on the relative value of celibacy and marriage, and on the hierarchy of women and men.

HERMENEUTICAL ALTERNATIVES

The issue that confronts us, then, is whether the canon in any sense can be taken still as the primary and special context of theology. Do its boundaries influence the boundaries of theological reflection in a way that can be claimed of no other source? Even if the continuing experience and insight of the faith community that uses the Bible as its "scripture" provide material for theology and shape the way the canon is interpreted, are they still in a significant sense secondary to it, and accountable to it? This critical question has received two fundamentally different answers in recent biblical hermeneutics. One school attempts to preserve the presupposition of biblical integrity in reinterpreted form. Another challenges the finality of the authority of the canon, and brings to it external criteria.

"Canonical criticism" assumes the special normativity of the canon. It proceeds by extending, balancing, and contextualizing the meaning of certain theological positions within the canon by comparing them with others. The premise is that there is in principle a coherence at some level of positions whose relative diversity still is not denied. The foremost representative of this approach is the Old Testament scholar Brevard Childs. In *Biblical Theology in Crisis*,[9] he first criticizes the failure of the biblical theology movement of the 1940s and 1950s to take seriously the possibility that historical critical methods present a serious challenge to biblical "unity." Yet Childs believes in the end that a commitment to the canon as a whole as a norm for theology is viable.[10] What the canon makes possible is "a dialectical process of interpretation" of texts and books in the light of one another,[11] a process that presupposes a "faith claim" that the two Testaments can be combined as "compatible" witnesses to divine reality.[12] For instance, Childs shows how the impression of sex as dangerous folly given in Proverbs 7, via an encounter of a young man with an adulteress, is modified elsewhere in the same biblical book by an admonition to cultivate the satisfactions of fidelity (Proverbs 5); is qualified still further in a positive direction by the erotic imagery of the Song of Songs; and finally how the Old Testament view of marriage generally qualifies the decidedly negative perspective of 1 Corinthians 7. Childs insists not only that the theologian must attend to the "full range" of biblical witnesses on a particular issue, but also that these witnesses will have an "inner movement."[13]

In his more recent *Introduction to the Old Testament as Scripture*, Childs explains that it is the *final* (i.e., canonical) form of a text that is normative, rather than any stage in its prehistory that may be recoverable by methods of historical reconstruction. This final form is significant because it alone represents the definitive witness to the believing community's experience with God. It is only in the final form that the "normative history has reached an end," and can "exercise an authority on the community of faith."[14]

Ethicists or exegetes such as Larry Rasmussen and Bruce Birch echo Child's hermeneutical principles and his explicit presupposition of canonical integrity when they insist that any text or theme must be considered in the canonical "framework of control," which measures ongoing theological reflection and tradition.[15] The approach of the New Testament scholar Raymond E. Brown is similar insofar as he enjoins the interpreter, employing historical-critical methods, to attend to the meaning a passage has in a book taken as a whole, and to the meaning that emerges when that book is incorporated with other books in the canon, including both the Old and New Testaments.[16]

A position that reflects Childs's commitment to the canon, but that moves further toward the incorporation of other sources, is that of David Kelsey.[17] He insists on the interdependence of canonical authority, the common life of the church which appeals to it, and the theologian's "biblical construals" of how God is present in the community. He also is more reticent about claiming that diverse theological positions yielded by passages, books, or in the Old Testament by strands of authorship, can be combined as complementary. Yet he too concludes that the control Scripture provides on theology and community resides ultimately in the canon. The pattern and relations of materials in the canon establish the "outside limits" of theological positions, and also their "determinate possibilities."[18] A more tenuous grasp on canonical cohesiveness is offered by James Dunn. Addressing himself specifically to the New Testament problem, he argues that the distinctive and unifying thread is simply the commitment of all New Testament authors to the identity of the man Jesus of Nazareth with the exalted and soon to return Lord. This identity is interpreted, however, in irreducibly diverse ways.[19]

Those who endorse the counterapproach consider such efforts to retain canonical authority by restoring unity to be futile. They distinguish levels of biblical authority, usually with the aid of a theological criterion not derived directly from the Bible itself. This method results in a "canon within the canon," that is, with the selection of key texts, books, themes, or authors that control the interpretation, and by which some parts of the canon are considered less normative or nonnormative. This selection is understood to be necessary to any coherent connection between diverse biblical materials and contemporary understanding.

Rejecting the presuppositions both of canonical integrity and of its exclusive authority, the biblical scholar James Barr recently has asserted that "biblical theology," as the clarification of theological positions in the Bible, is only one component of the constructive theological task. And it is not necessarily the decisive one. The factors "relevant" to theology "include systematic questions, moral considerations and philosophical perspectives which lie beyond the scope of any biblical theology."[20] Meaningful theological interpretations of the canon require a choice of priorities within it. "What people call an inner 'canon' is really a principle of theological organization. . . ." "Something extrinsic, extra-textual, e.g., a core of historical events . . . the external events, or thoughts about which the canonical text tells" may also be substituted for this inner canon. The selection of such a focus of theological interpretation may be criticized for being historically unfounded or incompatible with some nonbiblical standard of meaning or importance, but *not* simply because the hermeneutical key lies outside the biblical texts themselves.[21] Against Childs, Barr argues that canonical criticism represents a longing for "hermeneutical certainty" within definite boundaries, but that to assert that such certainty can be provided by the canon does not make it fact.[22]

A more blunt rejection of the canon as a norm for faith, theology, and ethics is represented by Jack Sanders. In *Ethics in the New Testament*, he adopts the radical stance that New Testament ethical positions, premised on a particular eschatology, are "alien and foreign to this day and age." From their "bondage" we must be "freed": "Tradition and precedent must not be allowed to stand in the way of what is humane and right."[23] He says that the subordinationist *Haustafel* passages in the later Pauline tradition reduce Christian ethics to good citizenship and endorse the social institutions of patriarchy and slavery, which Christians today find loathsome. Sanders readily acknowledges not only the necessity of choosing within the canon a privileged canon opposed to other biblical materials, but also that of the application by "each age" of "its own criteria to Christian tradition," criteria that extend beyond distinctively Christian resources. In this book Sanders does not elaborate with any specificity the nature of these criteria or their method of application.[24]

One senses a greater commitment to continuity with the biblical tradition in the analysis of an author like Paul Hanson, who rejects "canonical criticism" but seems to relocate canonical integrity from the level of substance to that of form.[25] His theory of biblical interpretation is of an interesting type. While rejecting some special theological and ethical positions represented in the Bible, he uses the structure of the dynamic between positions as a model for contemporary hermeneutics. We will see that this concern to understand the normativity of the dynamic *structures* and interpretative *patterns* within the canon, even while rejecting some of its substantive theological and moral conclusions, characterizes several authors. These refuse to identify with "canonical criticism." But in a less direct sense they use the canon to shape their hermeneutic of the diversity and even inadequacy of theologies within it.

Hanson resolves the problem of the diversity of Scripture in a manner recalling Barr. Hanson extends the revelatory activity of God to the church tradition. But he claims that subsequent tradition follows the biblical tradition itself in developing by means of "form/reform" and "vision/revision" polarities. Hanson appears clearly motivated by a concern to avoid some standard outcomes of treating the canon as sole authority, such as hierarchical views of men and women. Thus he insists that the latter, more dynamic, poles must be given special consideration in theology, since the status quo generally has the weight of familiarity on its side. A dynamic view of Christianity's "confessional heritage" emerges from the dynamic of Scripture itself. In this view, the tradition should recognize and criticize those historically particular confessions of faith that are inadequate to later experience, even if they are in the canon. Indeed, Hanson says,

> The desire to remove the various offenses of the Bible, that is, to rewrite the Bible so as to reflect a contemporary theology, participates in the desire to create a biblical proof text for our own theological position. The Bible has always resisted that, for

the Bible cannot provide proof, whether to the slave owner, the liberationist, the socialist, the capitalist, or to anyone else.[26]

Similar interpretations were reached earlier by Joseph Blenkin-sopp,[27] Paul Ricoeur,[28] and James Sanders.[29] Sanders differs in that he claims explicitly that his affirmation of an "inner dialectic which provides the parameters for any discussion today" is consistent with canonical criticism because it shares the presupposition that "the problem of biblical authority must be broached in full canonical context."[30] This reveals the possible ground of rapprochement between the two methods.

Keeping in mind the controversy between canonical criticism and a biblical hermeneutics that accords equal authority to extrabiblical resources, it may be most fruitful to see the "authority of the canon as a whole" primarily in terms of its overall forms and of the types of witness it includes. That is to say, in terms of the *patterns* of interaction, complementarity, and tension which characterize the religious heritage preserved in the canon and reappropriated in contact with it. The understanding of "canonical authority as authoritative pattern, structure, or form" can be contrasted to "substantive canonical authority," or the attempt to require that the canon as a whole function in the "authorization" of particular moral conclusions. On particulars, certain biblical positions or combinations of them may be incomplete, inadequate, or wrong. While it will be helpful to look for guidance in evaluation by critically examining and juxtaposing biblical texts or positions (e.g., on the role of women), it will not be assumed that these positions can and must offer definitive answers. Helpful here is the comment of Kelsey, who recognizes both that the canon is authoritative in a special way, as a somehow "final" form of faith expression, and that that authority is dependent on the tradition. Although the normativity of Scripture for theology consists in its being "*determinate* enough to impose some controls on what theologians may say in the name of elucidating Christian faith and life,"[31] the determinate and controlling aspect of Scripture is not its "conceptual content" but the "patterns" in biblical texts and the relations among those patterns, and of the patterns to the "whole" which is the canon.[32] The still disputed question is whether those patterns are likely to be patterns of substantive meaning as well as of structural interaction. I maintain that while not every substantive ethical problem can be resolved by the canon, nonetheless some of its central meaning patterns will continue to inform and illuminate Christian experience.

THE CANON AND ETHICS:
SAMPLES OF INTERPRETATION

Recent books adducing biblical evidence in favor of ethical positions demonstrate the ramifications of theories about whether the Bible is authoritative precisely as "canon," in what way, and in what relation to other sources. Again, primary concerns are the diversity within the canon, whether biblical positions lose authority in proportion to their determination by socio-historical context, and whether such positions can be evaluated by criteria outside the Bible. Such criteria could be those yielded by subsequent communities or those which lie "behind" the texts as their historical condition of possibility.

Thomas Ogletree's *The Use of the Bible in Christian Ethics*[33] is an example of Barr's point that no theological interpretation of the Bible can proceed without some principle of organization of the "canonical" materials that assigns some of them priority. Yet it is just as well an example of the common central insight of the canonical critics, and, less explicitly, of those who find canonical normativity in the patterns of relationship of varied positions within it. This central insight is that the Bible is uniquely authoritative for theology, but that its authority does not preclude the critical relation of other sources to the Bible, especially to its specific, substantive, theological, and ethical positions. The same can be said of Schüssler Fiorenza's *In Memory of Her*, although Schüssler Fiorenza places considerably more emphasis on the importance of a critical attitude toward the Bible. Two other authors, Krister Stendahl and Robin Scroggs, develop ethical positions on specific issues which depart from the authority of canonical parallels. Stendahl claims that biblical positions must be qualified by new insights; Scroggs claims that certain biblical evaluations are relative to historical and cultural contexts that no longer obtain.

Ogletree's fundamental approach to hermeneutics is indebted to phenomenological philosophy. He announces his project as a search

for a "common ground for understanding" between the authors of
biblical texts and later interpreters. This ground does not involve
the reduction of normative meaning to original meaning, but is one
on which "we do place our own convictions at risk."[34] The result
is a shared meaning which is also an enlarged meaning, the creation
of the interpreter as well as of the author.[35] Ogletree adds substance
to Hans-Georg Gadamer's hermeneutical ideal of fusion by elucidating as its condition of possibility certain common but "historically
contextualized" features of moral experience.[36]

Several features of this hermeneutic are intriguing in light of the
foregoing discussion. First, Ogletree uses a nonbiblical, philosophical resource to understand both the Bible and the experience of its
interpreters. Second, when Ogletree uses Scripture, he focuses on
those parts of the canon that are congenial to his thesis. He claims
that these parts are central, but not necessarily that his thesis draws
from *every* part of the canon. His choice of materials is directed by
a particular theme, that of "eschatology."[37]

> The primary challenge to Christian ethics is to find suitable ways
> of articulating the import of the eschatology which figures in the
> biblical materials.[38]

Eschatology, however, functions as a "meaning horizon" rather than
a substantive religious or moral notion. Thus Ogletree is able to
avoid Sanders's conclusion that because modern eschatologies differ
from biblical ones, the latter, and the ethics associated with them,
are irrelevant to the former. Third, the canonical form of the biblical
texts, and the ways they historically have represented eschatological
insights, is for Ogletree neither the most important nor the final
moment in the transmission of tradition.[39] Nonetheless, he claims
that the diversity in the Bible is brought together in a "thematic
unity, that is, the unfolding identity of a people." It is in relation
to this theme that eschatology emerges as a biblically essential qualification. The collective memory of past events is transformed by
future expectations and their impact upon the present.[40] In the New
Testament in particular, the sense of history is marked by "a conviction that the new age has already dawned."[41]

For Ogletree, then, the challenge of the Bible for Christian ethics
lies not in a particular moral notion, imperative, or code, but in the

historical realization of moral experience in such a way that the
dialectic between past memory and eschatological horizon both realized and future, is maintained. In ways generally resembling Blenkinsopp, James Sanders, Hanson, and Ricoeur, Ogletree locates biblical authority in a relation between basic horizons of communal
self-understanding, rather than in particular religious and theological formulations. It is presumed that specific religious symbols, faith
articulations, and theological conceptualizations may well be fruitful
for contemporary theology, but they also may be modified by other
biblical and extrabiblical insights. It is important that Ogletree's
theme of eschatology has very definite implications for the more
specific forms of normative ethics. The "common ground" of biblical
and contemporary faith is "some degree of alienation" from the larger
society, and "deep involvement" with an alternative community.[42]
These requisite features of Christian ethics will be historically con-
cretized in different ways. Particular Christian communities must
furnish the substantive meaning that this alienation and this involvement must have for their own social, political, and religious
situations. Fidelity to the canonical theme of eschatology does not
require appropriation of every specific biblical expression of it, but
more fundamentally that the religious community as historical tradition also be understood critically as called to the kingdom.

THE CANON
AND APPLIED ETHICS

Schüssler Fiorenza offers provocative discussion of the authority
of Scripture in relation to a specific social and moral problem, the
role of women, in *In Memory of Her*. She attempts the justification
of selective criteria with which to use biblical materials regarding
this issue, but her method has ramifications for the authority of the
canon in general. The nature of Schüssler Fiorenza's proposal is
made explicit by the book's subtitle: *A Feminist Theological Reconstruction of Christian Origins*. She argues that certain trajectories
within the New Testament, for example, accommodation to subordinationist cultural institutions for the sake of the Christian sect's
survival, are a departure from the "discipleship of equals" originally
called into being by the gospel and realized in the ministry of Jesus.
The inconsistencies in the New Testament view of women (e.g.,

Gal. 3:28 versus 1 Cor. 14:34–36) manifest an early struggle over the leadership of women, and the androcentric process of transmission perpetuated by the victors, rather than the full historical situation of women in the first Christian communities. For Schüssler Fiorenza, it is of crucial importance to "move from androcentric text to the social-religious life of women," and thus to use historical methods to "seek the social reality producing these texts."[43] What Schüssler Fiorenza understands to be normative in the canon are those passages or visions that reflect the egalitarianism of Jesus' ministry. Thus one norm of biblical interpretation is a historical reality which lies "behind" the Bible even if revealed through it. Further, the basis from which the "revelatory canon" within the New Testament may be separated out from degenerative images is the concrete struggle of women against oppression and their experience of liberation.[44] The paradigm for understanding Scripture is not "unchanging archetype" but "historical prototype," that is, a historically concrete model which will be transformed rather than reproduced within the "ongoing history" of the Christian community.[45]

This paradigm is important because it permits the biblical critic to retain Scripture—the "revelatory canon" within Scripture—as a norm while presupposing significant flexibility in its function as authority for theology. Scripture as "prototype" is not a fixed form with rigid contours into which all other expressions of Christian theology and practice must be forced. It is an initial model which can be improved, refined, and reshaped, even though future designs should bear a recognizable resemblance to the original.

In a later publication, Schüssler Fiorenza stresses even more clearly the need to replace a biblical "hermeneutics of consent" with one "of suspicion." She resists the notion that it is the aim of biblical interpretation simply to "fuse" a contemporary horizon of meaning with a patriarchal biblical one. Instead, she insists that an adequate hermeneutic must adopt an advocacy stance for the oppressed, particularly women, whose liberation does *not* emerge as a clear biblical concern.[46]

At first view, Schüssler Fiorenza's "feminist critical hermeneutics of liberation" seems to amount to a proposal both that part of the traditional canon is authoritative and part is not, and that the historical reality of the community Jesus originally gathered around him is recoverable by applying historical-critical methods to the New Testament in its canonical form. The latter suggestion poses not only the problem of the nature of evidence for the historical basis of New Testament images and theologies, but also that of the connection historical information about Jesus has or ought to have to the normative claims of faith. We will return to this matter shortly. On the issue of canon, Schüssler Fiorenza certainly is eschewing any faith presupposition that biblical positions, in essence or accidents, can be harmonized, integrated, or unified around a common theme, by virtue of which they all enjoy, despite apparent diversity, authoritative status.

From another perspective, however, Schüssler Fiorenza implies that both androcentric and egalitarian strands are united *insofar as* they reveal an original discipleship of equals as their condition of possibility.[47] Emergent patriarchy in the New Testament reflects precisely a struggle against the vision of cohumanity embodied in Jesus' ministry. Attempts to reinstitutionalize patriarchy in a Christian mode bespeak exactly the response of human sinfulness that attests to the authenticity of Jesus' preaching of the gospel, of God's will for the salvation of fallen humanity. On the one hand, it is true that any notion of "unity" may become so loose that its usefulness is seriously diminished if it can include opposites of meaning under the tags "affirmation" and "reaction." On the other, while Schüssler Fiorenza does not speak explicitly of any canonical unity of positive and negative texts, she does assert that the negative in fact presupposes that life and those events that make both sorts of texts possible. She thus implies a unity of opposites in a common condition of possibility, which differs from a random collection of disparate positions that happen to contradict one another.

In addition to her use of the canon itself to mount a critique of canonical materials, Schüssler Fiorenza appeals to a source, or more precisely, an experience, which is not "extrinsic" to Christianity, but which also is not to be identified simply with "Christian canon" or "tradition." That is the experience of liberation; liberation is a hermeneutical principle for distinguishing true from false, genuine from inauthentic, portrayals of Jesus. Schüssler Fiorenza makes neither the content nor the criteria of the "liberating" experience explicit, and so leaves inconclusive the problem of control in the use of liberation as a standard of scriptural authority. Liberating for whom? Who is to decide whether one woman's (or man's) claimed experience of liberation is illusory, incomplete, or disingenuous? Despite this ambiguity, Schüssler Fiorenza has considerable collegial support behind her insistence both that interpretation requires criteria beyond the canon, and that biblical religion is not a meaningful norm for the ongoing church if it is envisioned as something closed, static, and finally ahistorical. In the final analysis, it may be that Schüssler Fiorenza's norm of liberation is not completely extrinsic. Insofar as she connects it with Jesus' "discipleship of equals," it is informed by biblical models of normative human relationship. To some extent she does understand a concern for women's oppressed status to emerge from the New Testament. If so, this is not a shortcoming, but an evidence of the dialectical nature of Christian self-definition which it would be helpful to acknowledge more directly.

Other interpreters, deciding that their choice lies between canonical positions and the consistency of Christian teaching with modern experience, entirely give up reinterpreting the authority or unity of the canon at some other level. The experience of the subsequent faith community becomes an equally important norm, and may be used to discriminate among biblical positions. The dialectic of authority cuts two ways; the canon is not necessarily "primary" in relation to later faith commitments. Krister Stendahl, taking sexuality as a case in point, concludes that there are some areas in which the theologian must take issue with the fairly consistent testimony of Scripture. Stendahl states this even more strongly than Schüssler Fiorenza:

> The basic impression of women's subordination in practically all respects is part of the biblical tradition in its main thrust. The exceptions only prove the rule.[48]

Stendahl suggests that the church "should not be so anxious to close a lot of issues," since, not only are there "new data,"[49] but some parts of Scripture belong to human "fallenness."[50] Even central biblical authors like Paul occasionally fail "to live up to" insights that are contained elsewhere in the Scriptures, even in their own writings.[51] Stendahl closely resembles Schüssler Fiorenza in challenging

not only some specific biblical teachings, but also certain fundamental pictures of male and female relationships that are found in
the Bible, and in attributing the nonnormativity of the latter to
human fallenness, which he admits is reflected in the canon (e.g.,
1 Tim. 2:9–15). Neither author defines precisely the criteria of discrimination between redemptive and sinful, normative and nonnormative, canonical elements, but refers them to ongoing communal experience. This, for Schüssler Fiorenza, makes plain a
contrast between liberation and oppression in the canon itself; and,
for Stendahl, requires a broadening of what is theologically "authoritative" to include what is novel in Christian experience.

Another recent study poses the question of canon in relation to
the morality of homosexuality, taking up specifically the problem
of New Testament condemnations of homosexual activity.[52] Scroggs
concludes that these judgments "are not relevant to today's debate,"
primarily because, Scroggs argues, the type of sexual activity toward
which they are directed is the exploitative pederasty so prevalent in
the Greco-Roman world. This author too allows contemporary experience to modify biblical authority. At a more general level,
Scroggs suggests that any biblical statements about ethics need to
meet two tests for continuing relevance: in addition to exhibiting a
"reasonable similarity" of context, they must be consonant with "the
heart" of theology and ethics in Scripture and in "the historical
church."[53] While Scroggs's two criteria are helpful in relating specific moral statements to the larger spheres of experience and tradition, they also present ambiguities. How precisely is it to be determined what is the "heart" of the biblical and ethical traditions of
Christianity, and which specific moral judgments are or are not
enduring expressions of it? As has been shown, many scholars dispute that there is any single substantive theme that lies at the core
of the biblical traditions. Moreover, what aspect of the referent of
a moral judgment is its "context" and how is the "reasonableness"
of similarity between two contexts to be ascertained? While the
specific contexts of biblical and modern discussion of homosexuality
are different, in that they have in view different sorts of homosexual
relationship, their broader contexts may have points in common.
An example is the Judeo-Christian commitment to heterosexual monogamy as the proper sphere of sexual activity. Finally, Scroggs's

commendable call for attention to the "major" theological and ethical themes of Scripture and tradition returns us to the question of canonical integrity, and to that of the critical function of the canon for tradition, including present communal experience.

THE HISTORICAL BASES OF
FAITH AND THEOLOGY

A common thread in all these discussions of whether it is Scripture as *canon* that is authoritative is the link of the "canonical" collection to the various historical communities that produced the biblical texts and so in a sense lie behind and beyond them. To what extent is the historical basis of the Bible—the history of Israel and of the actual events in which it saw God's actions, or the man Jesus and his first followers—the object of Christian faith and the ground of the Bible's continuing authority? For Schüssler Fiorenza, the normative character of Scripture goes back to the ministry of Jesus as the ultimate norm. Stendahl says that the interpreter must start with the historical author's intention, but that it is not necessarily normative; originality is of interest, but does not automatically confer authority. Others such as Jack Sanders and Scroggs have used historicity precisely to discount authority. And, for all, a fundamental problem is whether, if Scripture is constituted by the believing community's interpretations of historical events, not "historical records" in the modern sense, the historical basis of the canon is recoverable at all. Today's interpreter or theologian finds the path well trodden by those who engaged in or repudiate the "quest" (and "new quest") for the "historical Jesus." The quest for the historical Jesus was occasioned by the development of the historical sciences, which made it possible to make the Jesus of the Gospels the subject of historical-critical research.[54] It is a classic example of a perennial dilemma: how to construe the relation between Scripture, the events to which it refers, and its interpreters. As Günther Bornkamm has stated, "We possess no single word of Jesus and no single story of Jesus, no matter how incontestably genuine they may be, which do not embody at the same time the confession of the believing congregation, or at least are embedded therein."[55]

While few biblical scholars now would see the historical base for faith in Christ as the only important object of study, they obviously would not urge that faith and theology must be utterly independent of historical investigation, nor that it is dispensable to the self-understanding of the believer or the believing community.[56] Van A. Harvey accepts that the certitude of faith is not absolutely independent of the historical verification of its premises:

> It has been pointed out that while historical inquiry can never prove the belief that Jesus was the Son of God, it can nevertheless, cast doubts on it, at least in principle. For what if it were confirmed beyond a reasonable doubt that Jesus never lived or that he was not crucified or that his actual words were quite different in content and spirit from those preserved by the church?[57]

Not only Christianity but also Judaism is a religion whose very nature is to refer to historical communities and events, even though these are never rendered without the interpretation of faith.[58] To say that Israelite and Christian religion both interpret present experience in the light of past history, however, is to say two different things. While the historical focus of Christianity (or the New Testament) is the life of an individual man, that of Judaism (or the Old Testament) is the history of a people whose identity and career varied tremendously over several centuries. Furthermore, the life and teaching of Jesus of Nazareth, which the church remembers and proclaims, have for the church universally an authority that can be attributed in the same way to no single person or event in the Israelite history, not even to Moses, the exodus, or the making of the covenant at Sinai. This makes even more difficult any precise definition of the relation of the historical to the normativity of the canon in a way that would apply to the *whole* Christian Scripture.

As we have seen, scholars and interpreters of both Israelite and specifically Christian materials generally demonstrate interest in the original historical situation out of which and for which a text was written, and in the likely intention of its author and the impression made on those who first heard or read it. But they also are careful to distinguish such a meaning from that taken on for subsequent communities of interpretation. A primary concern is to uphold at the same time the legitimacy and importance of historical-critical research; and the freedom of theology to interpret biblical passages, books, or images in ways consonant with the contemporary experience of the faith community. The crucial question, whose answer is so elusive, is exactly how and to what degree the original meaning or its historical referent acts as a critical standard of subsequent interpretation.

Though these questions have not always been given completely satisfying answers, the mainstream of biblical scholars tends to support their legitimacy. All approaches are inadequate which either dichotomize or identify the *original* meaning, insofar as it is accessible; and the *subsequent* meanings which a text, or book, or image may take in its role as authoritative Scripture. Examples of such approaches are biblical fundamentalism, historicism, Bultmannian existentialism, structuralism, and, to an extent, literary criticism. Helpful here is Ogletree's suggestion, following Gadamer, that the original meaning challenges contemporary "preunderstanding" but that the *normative* meaning of a biblical position will result from a dialectic of author's and interpreter's "meaning horizons." A remaining question is the extent to which contact with the original horizon includes or is dependent upon some understanding of the actual persons, communities, and events that it framed.

HISTORICAL CRITERIA

Harvey makes the case that the separation of the historical Jesus from the kerygmatic Christ, to use Bultmann's phrases, is not only untenable, but oversimplistic, and perhaps impossible. Harvey's position is that the critical link between the Jesus of the historian and the Jesus of the believer is the memory-image of the actual, historical Jesus which all the New Testament communities share in common and on which they base their different interpretative christologies. This impression emphasizes and incorporates the elements of the historical Jesus which, in their *consistency*, are key for faith: his teaching, his acts, and his crucifixion. Insofar as the selective image is drawn from historical tradition, it in principle can be criticized by the historian, as can the biblical Christ, which also has a presumed relation to the facts grounding the recollected image.[59] At least the Christ of faith must be consistent with what the believing community remembered as significantly characteristic of the man Jesus, in whom they came to recognize the dawning of God's reign.

Biblical scholars adept with the tools of historical criticism have
been able to apply them constructively on the presupposition of
some such normative connection of the historical Jesus, at least to
a certain extent disclosed through the memories of primitive Christianity, and the Christ of the kerygma proclaimed by that community. Norman Perrin has pointed out that the New Testament
itself, especially Matthew, Mark, and Luke, is interested in the past,
in the life and death of the man Jesus, even as it reinterprets this
historical past with the motives of faith, so that "in the case of the
synoptic gospels this past dimension is dominant in the proclamation."[60] So consistency of the kerygmatic Christ with the Jesus of
history is a concern whose legitimacy is borne out within Scripture
itself. It might be said that the affirmation that the faith is *historically*
grounded is a constitutive element in the horizon with which the
Bible addresses its interpreters.

Both Perrin and Reginald Fuller have argued that key elements
in the historical message of Jesus can be reconstructed on the basis
of the New Testament, and have offered criteria for establishing
which saying or teachings can be traced back to authentic Jesus
material.[61] Perrin also has argued that the basic historical knowledge
of Jesus yielded by the New Testament is confirmed generally by
historical and non-Christian sources. For instance, "A fundamental
concern of Jesus was to bring together into a unified group those
who responded to his proclamation of the Kingdom of God irres-
pective of their sex, previous background or history."[62] What is the
theological (or, by extension, ethical) significance of such knowledge
of historical fact? Perrin states it in terms of a minimal criterion of
authenticity:

> The true kerygmatic Christ, the justifiable faith-image, is that
> consistent with the historical Jesus. The significance of the his-
> torical Jesus for Christian faith is that knowledge of this Jesus
> may be used as a means of testing the claims of the Christs pre-
> sented in the competing kerygmata to be Jesus Christ.[63]

Thus, as Barr indicated, the historical events that gave rise to the
canon may be used as an interpretive key. However, it would be a
mistake to see those events as genuinely "external," both because

they are accessible primarily through the canon and because the canon includes them as an integral part of its own meaning.

Although Schüssler Fiorenza distances herself from any "quest for the historical Jesus," her feminist critique of the canon is a good example of attention to the historical basis of faith. She claims that "the locus of revelation is not the androcentric text but the life and ministry of Jesus and the movement of women and men called forth by him," and urges that this ministry be recovered by "critical-historical methods."[64] Both positive and negative reactions to that original historical reality reflect a social, historical response to the Christian vision originating in Christ.[65] As she defines her understanding of the New Testament,

> It does not seek to distill the "historical Jesus" from the remembering interpretations of his first followers, nor does it accept their interpretation uncritically and without question. Therefore, whenever I speak here of Jesus I speak of him as his life and ministry is available to historical-critical reading of the earliest interpretations of the first Christians.[66]

One is reminded immediately not only of Harvey's distinction between the "historical Jesus" and the "memory image" of Jesus *but also* of the connection he construes between the two. Certainly Schüssler Fiorenza is right to abandon crude searches for the historical details of the life of the man, Jesus of Nazareth. But Harvey is persuasive in his argument, followed through by Perrin, that a sophisticated interpretation of the Christian interest in historical information about Jesus will acknowledge at the outset that such information is available primarily through the selective memory of primitive Christianity, and that, as Schüssler Fiorenza (and Perrin) seems to allow, it is that memory, grounded firmly in the historical reality, that cuts through valid and invalid kerygmas. She claims that early Christian egalitarian movements are to be "glimpsed" *through* the New Testament itself, even though not all the theological elaborations it contains are normative; the androcentric trajectories have as their very premise the participation of women in community leadership.[67] Thus the canon is brought together as an authoritative whole in that both its oppressive and its liberating images reveal as their historical condition of possibility the ministry of Jesus and the egalitarian communities of early Christianity.

CONCLUSION

In some sense, any decision to use Scripture as an authority for theology is a faith decision, that is, one that involves a commitment to the reliability of that authority, a commitment grounded in one's experience within the community shaped by Scripture. The authority of Scripture does not rest on any empirical or logical demonstration that Scripture, in its several parts or as a whole, can support *only* the sort of theology or religious faith that is "authentic," "liberating," or "healing," that is, congruent with one's experience of God, and with the understanding of God coherent with extra-biblical insights. The knowledge that Scripture *does* support this sort of theology and faith is a knowledge at which the individual and community arrive through a critical process of appropriating and using Scripture, while at the same time having always already been formed and directed by it. To say that the decision to use the canon as an authority is a faith decision is, then, not to say that it is arbitrary. Rather, it is warranted by the recognition that this religious literature and these images have in an essential way actually shaped the community and engendered communal experience that is "redemptive," that is, healing, reunifying, and liberating. Although not all religious images or theological portrayals presented in Scripture are redemptive if isolated, the Bible is nonetheless redemptive in a way that is recognizable, if difficult to define.

One thing that can be asserted clearly is that the disclosive and redemptive character of the Christian Bible is closely associated with key historical traditions, events, and persons. The Christian God is a God revealed and active in history, in the lives, accomplishments, failures, joys, sufferings, and deaths of creatures divinely made, sustained, judged, and called. God is known in Israel's history as a scattered, racially linked, and oppressed aggregation of nomads; as an ancient Near Eastern nation; and as conquered exiles with common racial, religious, and national roots. In the New Testament, the focus on the historical locus of the faith experience is much more pointed: the life of Jesus, preserved in the common memory on which the diverse canonical interpretations of Jesus' meaning are premised. The "teaching of Jesus," best described as continually "re-presented" in the canon rather than "recoverable" through it, furnishes from within the canon a critical norm to be applied to the canon. The commitment of faith is that we do in fact intend to regard the teaching, ministry, and person of Jesus, as well as the historically actualized covenant of Yahweh with Israel, as authoritative because they make possible and continue to encourage a truthful relationship between God and humanity.

The problem in extending any historical criterion of faith and theology to the Hebrew Scriptures, obviously, is that there is no one historical figure or original author whose life, words, and deeds are accepted as absolutely paradigmatic. The authors of the documentary strands of the Pentateuch, for example, have at best the status of Paul, or the authors of the Gospels, not that of Jesus, to whom the Gospels and epistles lead back as their historical point of genesis. This reality is no doubt partly responsible for the fact that primarily interpreters whose special area is the Old Testament (Hebrew Bible) have explained the authority of the canon in terms of its structures or patterns. It is worth noting that this theory does assert the importance of the historical basis of the Scriptures, since the relations of materials within them are taken as reflections of the historical career of the faith community and of its dialectical self-understanding. The canon provides a model for theology and ethics by communicating the counterpoint and balance of positions actually formulated in different historical periods or by different sub-traditions.

New Testament scholars tend in contrast to devote more attention to the possible authority of historical events or persons, for instance, Jesus, his ministry, his teachings, or those of St. Paul. Both approaches permit the canon to be used in some sense as a unique and privileged context of theological reflection. Yet representatives of both agree that not *all* substantive theological positions in the canon are normative in the sense of requiring incorporation into or reconciliation with contemporary interpretation. Thus, it can be allowed that the articulation of specific theological and ethical positions will require insights "extrinsic" in a sense to the canon: the subsequent tradition of the faith community; the actual, describable past and present of the human community and human individuals;

and normative reflection on the sort of virtues, lives, and communities that would best fulfill humanity.

As James Gustafson has concluded, "Scripture *alone* is never the final court of appeal for Christian ethics."[68] It seems to me that this judgment cannot but be persuasive once it is recognized that not only does an interpretative reconstruction of foundational events occur already within Scripture, but that a determinate religious, cultural, and historical context always is and has been required for the reception of God's Word by those whose hearing is made possible by God's Spirit. The Scriptures can be the *norma normans non normata* (the norm which is normative without being subject to any norm) of theology only in a nuanced or modified sense; it is the original and primary standard, but its very perception as authoritative standard is contingent upon the continuing life of the church that it engenders; comprehension of the actual human situation to which it speaks; and some innately human capacity to criticize that situation and envision a standard of "humanity" that transcends it.

NOTES

1. Helpful critical discussions of biblical authority are included in the "Selected Bibliography" in categories A. Biblical Hermeneutics and B. The Bible and Ethics.

2. James D. G. Dunn, *Unity and Diversity in the New Testament: An Inquiry into the Character of Earliest Christianity* (Philadelphia: Westminster Press; London: SCM Press, 1977), 4.

3. Ibid., 376. Dunn judges, "Perhaps then the tragedy of early Catholicism was its failure to realize that the biggest heresy of all is the insistence that there is only one ecclesiastical obedience, only one orthodoxy" (p. 366).

4. More than one commentator has remarked that there is more than one way to "adduce" biblical "evidence" (James M. Gustafson, "The Place of Scripture in Christian Ethics: A Methodological Study," in *Theology and Christian Ethics* [New York: Pilgrim Press, 1974], 130–35, first published in *Interpretation* 24/4 [1974]; Bruce C. Birch and Larry L. Rasmussen, *Bible and Ethics in the Christian Life* [Minneapolis: Augsburg Pub. House, 1976], 84, 114–17). Gustafson set the parameters of much subsequent discussion among ethicists when he described four models of which he prefers the last: (1) Scripture as revealed moral law; (2) Scripture as a source of moral ideals; (3) Scripture as a narrative about situations and actions analogous to our own, and in the light of which we can discern God's will for us; (4) Scripture as a witness to a "great variety" of values, norms, and principles which can be applied to present situations

only with the help of other sources of moral insight. Birch and Rasmussen claim that the primary moral function of Scripture is to form Christian community and identity but also add that biblical materials can aid formulation of rules and principles via (1) positive prescriptions, (2) establishing outer boundaries of conduct, and (3) locating the burden of proof and the justifiable exceptions to a norm (p. 117). Ten years subsequent to its publication of Gustafson's essay, *Interpretation* published an issue oriented by the theme of Bible and Christian ethics (34/4 [1980]). Stanley Hauerwas, noted for his work on the relation of the Christian "story" to the formation of community and of character, contributed "The Moral Authority of Scripture: The Politics and Ethics of Remembering," 356–70. James F. Childress argues that Scripture is also important in the formulation of specific moral arguments, in "Scripture and Christian Ethics: Some Reflections on the Role of Scripture in Moral Deliberation and Justification," 371–80.

5. Much controversy revolves around the terms "inspiration," "revelation," and "inerrancy." The debates are sensitive and involve distinctions of fine points. I work with the presupposition that the biblical texts are divinely authored in the sense that it is God who initiates and controls the process through which they are produced. God is the "author" of the people of God and their faith and thus indirectly of the documents through which that faith is expressed. (See Avery Dulles, "The Authority of Scripture: A Catholic Perspective," in *Scripture in the Jewish and Christian Traditions: Authority, Interpretation, Relevance*, ed. Frederick E. Greenspahn [Nashville: Abingdon Press, 1982], 24.) A biblical author is inspired in the sense that he produces an integral communication, a letter, for instance, in which the acts and will of God are faithfully revealed. However, to claim that every detail of that integral work is free from error of any sort, whether natural, scientific, or historical, would be to deny either that there is a cooperation between divine and human authorship, or that human beings are intrinsically limited. Even further, I would agree with Raymond E. Brown that the biblical authors had religious limitations as well. It is precisely for this reason that Christian tradition has depended on the *canonical collection* as its authority. It depends on complementary texts and books within the canon, patterns within those books, and relations among patterns in the canon as a whole, as the critical norm of Scripture for theology. (See Brown, *The Critical Meaning of the Bible* [New York: Paulist Press, 1981], viii–44.)

6. The Christian "canon" was established around the fourth century, as the result of a process of common usage. By the fourth century, the same twenty-seven books of the New Testament were referred to and used with consistency. The Roman Catholic Church did not conclusively *define* the canon until the Council of Trent (1546). There remains a discrepancy between Catholic, on the one hand, and Protestant and Jewish, on the other, definitions of the Old Testament or Hebrew Bible. To the thirty-nine books of Protestants and Jews, Catholics add Judith, Tobit, Ecclesiasticus (Sirach), Wisdom, 1 and 2 Mac-

cabees, and Baruch, making a total of forty-six. These seven were included in the Greek Septuagint, but were not actually regarded as "canon" by the Jews. For more technical discussions of canonicity, see A. C. Sundberg, Jr., "Canon of the NT," *Interpreter's Dictionary of the Bible*, supp. vol., ed. Keith Crim (Nashville: Abingdon Press, 1976), 136–40; D.N. Freedman, "Canon of the OT," ibid., 130–36; James C. Turro and Raymond E. Brown, "Canonicity," *Jerome Biblical Commentary*, ed. Raymond E. Brown, Joseph A. Fitzmyer, Roland E. Murphy (Englewood Cliffs, N.J.: Prentice-Hall, 1968), 515–34.

7. Ernst Käsemann, *Essays on New Testament Themes*, trans. W. J. Montague (London: SCM Press, 1964; Philadelphia: Fortress Press, 1982); cf. Brevard Childs, *Biblical Theology in Crisis*. (Philadelphia: Westminster Press, 1970), 69–70.

8. Elisabeth Schüssler Fiorenza, *In Memory of Her: A Feminist Theological Reconstruction of Christian Origins* (New York: Crossroad, 1983), xv.

9. Childs, *Biblical Theology in Crisis*.

10. "The Scriptures of the church provide the authoritative and definitive word that continues to shape and enliven the church" (Childs, *Biblical Theology in Crisis*, 100). The canon provides "a context, different from both Testaments, in which the Christian church continues to wrestle in every new age with the living God" (p. 113).

11. Ibid., 113.

12. Ibid., 111.

13. Ibid., 132.

14. Brevard Childs, *Introduction to the Old Testament as Scripture* (Philadelphia: Fortress Press, 1979), 76.

15. Birch and Rasmussen, *Bible and Ethics*, 175–77.

16. Brown, *Critical Meaning in the Bible*, 30–31.

17. David H. Kelsey, *The Uses of Scripture in Recent Theology* (Philadelphia: Fortress Press, 1975).

18. Ibid., 182–97. Kelsey borrows from Robert C. Johnson to offer the theory that Scripture functions as authority within a *discrimen*, that is, within "a configuration of criteria" which are "reciprocal" (p. 160). In general terms, the configuration or discrimen is the conjunction of certain actual uses of Scripture within the church and the continuing, active presence of God within the common life of the community. The use of Scripture in any particular theological position will depend on the theologian's "imaginative construal" of the mode of God's presence among the faithful, and the way in which that presence correlates with the use of Scripture by the church. Kelsey suggests that Scripture is "authoritative" or "normative" for the church in a *functional* sense. "Part of what it means to call a text or set of texts 'scripture' is that its uses in certain ways in the common life of the Christian community are *essential* to establishing and preserving the community's identity" (p. 89).

19. Dunn, *Unity and Diversity in the New Testament*, 29–32, 56–59.

20. James Barr, *Holy Scripture: Canon, Authority, Criticism* (Philadelphia: Westminster Press; London: SCM Press, 1983), 119.

21. Ibid., 71–72.

22. Ibid., 145–47.

23. Jack T. Sanders, *Ethics in the New Testament* (Philadelphia: Fortress Press, 1975), 130.

24. Sanders, *Ethics in the New Testament*, 88–90 (quotes from p. 88).

25. Paul Hanson, *The Diversity of Scripture: A Theological Interpretation*, Overtures to Biblical Theology 11 (Philadelphia: Fortress Press, 1983).

26. Ibid., 104.

27. Joseph Blenkinsopp, *Prophecy and Canon: A Contribution to the Study of Jewish Origins* (Notre Dame and London: Univ. of Notre Dame Press, 1977). Blenkinsopp tells us that "if we are to find a unitary principle of interpretation it will not be by elevating one postulate to a unique status but by examining the relations between different postulates within the context of the canon as a whole" (p. 140). A thesis that Hanson seems to follow is that both tradition and prophetic criticism are crucial to the existence of the religious community. The inclusion of both in the canon provides a model for that community. "Our study of the canon has led to the conclusion that no one interpretation of the tradition can be accorded final and definitive status. The presence of prophecy as an essential part of the canon means that it will always be possible and necessary to remold the tradition as a source of life-giving power" (p. 152).

28. See Lewis S. Mudge's "Introduction" to Paul Ricoeur's *Essays on Biblical Interpretation* (Philadelphia: Fortress Press, 1983), especially pp. 19–22. Mudge also refers the reader to "The Hermeneutics of Symbols: I," in Paul Ricoeur, *The Conflict of Interpretations: Essays on Hermeneutics*, ed. Don Ihde (Evanston, Ill.: Northwestern Univ. Press, 1974).

29. James A. Sanders, *Torah and Canon* (Philadelphia: Fortress Press, 1972).

30. Ibid., xv.

31. Kelsey, *Uses of Scripture*, 192.

32. Ibid., 193–97.

33. Thomas W. Ogletree, *The Use of the Bible in Christian Ethics: A Constructive Essay* (Philadelphia: Fortress Press, 1983).

34. Ibid., 1–2.

35. Ibid., 3, 176.

36. Ogletree argues that moral existence and agency have certain constant characteristics: intentionality, intersubjectivity, and continuity, framed by "the question of the meaning of being." These will be emphasized and articulated diversely in different historical contexts. For summaries of these points, see *Use of the Bible in Christian Ethics*, 40–41.

37. Eschatology is chosen as a centrally biblical way of answering "the question of the meaning of being" (Ogletree, *Use of the Bible in Christian Ethics*, 193).

38. Ibid., 117.

39. Ibid., 9.

40. Ibid., 69, 75–76.
41. Ibid., 87.
42. Ibid., 182.
43. Schüssler Fiorenza, *In Memory of Her*, 59.
44. Ibid., 32.
45. Ibid., 33–34.
46. Elisabeth Schüssler Fiorenza, "Contemporary Biblical Scholarship: Its Roots, Present Understandings, and Future Directions," in *Modern Biblical Scholarship: Its Impact on Theology and Proclamation*, ed. Francis A. Eigo, O.S.A. (Villanova, Pa.: Villanova Univ. Press, 1984), 21–22.
47. In Schüssler Fiorenza's words,

> Insofar as androcentric biblical texts not only reflect their patriarchal cultural environment but also continue to allow a glimpse of the early Christian movements as a discipleship of equals, the reality of women's engagement and leadership in these movements precedes the androcentric injunctions for women's role and behavior. Women who belonged to a submerged group in antiquity could develop leadership in the emerging Christian movement which, as a discipleship of equals, stood in tension and conflict with the patriarchal ethos of the Greco-Roman world. (*In Memory of Her*, 35)

48. Krister Stendahl, "Ancient Scripture in the Modern World," in *Scripture in the Jewish and Christian Traditions*, 206. Stendahl, however, is not satisfied with an approach that attempts a "gradation" in the canon, based for instance on dominical or apostolic primacy. Somewhat paradoxically, he adds,

> I am only saying that as the church lives with the Bible, what kind of view of Bible does it suggest if one has such a gradation as this: Jesus knows best, Paul knows well, and the secondary tradition is not of truly revelatory quality? I would think, being the kind of Christian I am, that it is really the Bible that is the guide for the life of the church. (p. 207)

An author who does seem to grant greater authority to earlier materials is Wolfgang Schrage. Writing on the New Testament view of the sexes, Schrage claims that it can be used to support either patriarchalism or feminism. Recognizing that one needs "certain standards and reference points," he selects "the Jesus tradition and Pauline passages" to be used as critical authorities against certain faulty New Testament developments. Thus Schrage uses the New Testament as a critic against itself, without, however, fully clarifying his method of selection of the "canon within the canon" (Erhard S. Gerstenberger and Wolfgang Schrage, *Woman and Man* [Nashville: Abingdon Press, 1981], 113–14).
49. Stendahl, "Ancient Scripture in the Modern World," 211. In his earlier study, directed toward a reconsideration of women's ordination in the Church of Sweden, Stendahl argues that rigid adherence to first-century practice, as discovered through historical method, is a "modern heresy." He advises that

the events of the New Testament, including the event of Christ, are history, the ongoing history of the community (*The Bible and the Role of Women: A Case Study in Hermeneutics* (Philadelphia: Fortress Press, 1966), 17, 21.

50. Ibid., 209.

51. Ibid., 208.

52. Robin Scroggs, *The New Testament and Homosexuality: Contextual Background for Contemporary Debate* (Philadelphia: Fortress Press, 1983). Scroggs's normative conclusions are suggested in the final chapter (pp. 123–29).

53. Ibid., 123.

54. Scholars such as Hermann S. Reimarus, David F. Strauss, Martin Kähler, Albert Schweitzer, and Rudolf Bultmann eventually made it clear that the Gospels are interpretive products of the early church which may not be compiled into a historically reliable account of Jesus' career. Norman Perrin, in *Rediscovering the Teaching of Jesus* (New York: Harper & Row; London: SCM Press, 1967), 207–48, provides a detailed and critically nuanced overview of the problem of the historical Jesus. Perrin includes an annotated bibliography. See also Carl Braaten and Roy Harrisville, eds., *The Historical Jesus* (Nashville: Abingdon Press, 1964); Dunn, *Unity and Diversity in the New Testament*, 205–16; and Leander E. Keck, *A Future for the Historical Jesus: The Place of Jesus in Preaching and Theology* (Philadelphia: Fortress Press, 1980; first published in 1971), esp. 17–46.

55. Günther Bornkamm, *Jesus of Nazareth* (New York: Harper & Row; London: Hodder & Stoughton, 1960), 4.

56. As Dunn observes, "a dominant concern of Gospel research over the past twenty years or so" has been to highlight points of continuity, such as eschatology which is at once realized and anticipatory, between the message of the historical Jesus that the kingdom is at hand, and the early Christian kerygma that it is in the person of Jesus that the kingdom is made present and accessible (*Unity and Diversity in the New Testament*, 207).

57. Van A. Harvey, *The Historian and the Believer: The Morality of Historical Knowledge and Christian Belief* (New York: Macmillan, 1966), 18. Ricoeur allows similarly that, beyond the religious "sense" to which biblical discourse testifies, "the question of the referential claims of these stories remains unavoidable" (Ricoeur's "Reply to Lewis S. Mudge," in *Essays on Biblical Interpretation*, 44).

58. Cf. ibid., 265.

59. Harvey, *The Historian and the Believer*, chap. 8, esp. pp. 265–81. Harvey refines the categories of the discussion by distinguishing four meanings of "Jesus of Nazareth": (1) Jesus "as he really was," who can never be fully described; (2) the "historical Jesus," i.e., as recoverable by the historian's means; (3) the selective and perspectival "memory impression" of the actual and historical Jesus, preserved by the first Christian communities as the basis on which the New Testament Christologies are built; and (4) "the biblical Christ," i.e., the theological interpretation of the memory-image from various perspectives, preserved in the canon as we now have it.

60. Perrin, *Rediscovering the Teaching of Jesus*, 234.

61. Reginald H. Fuller, *A Critical Introduction to the New Testament* (London: Gerald Duckworth & Co., 1966), 94–98; Norman Perrin, *The New Testament: An Introduction* (New York: Harcourt Brace Jovanovich, 1974), 281–82.

62. Perrin, *New Testament*, 288.

63. Ibid., 244. Keck finds criteria that isolate the *distinctive* teaching of Jesus unsatisfactory because they neglect the full picture of what is characteristic of Jesus. But he too finds the historical career of Jesus important because it alone can make the proclamation of Jesus as Lord convincing. The historical factuality of the crucifixion, for example, is a presupposition of trust in a Lord who conquers sin, suffering, and absurdity. "Congruence of life and word does not create proof . . . but it does give power to the word of witness without which preaching becomes propaganda" (Keck, *Future for the Historical Jesus*, 131).

64. Schüssler Fiorenza, *In Memory of Her*, 41.

65. Ibid., 92.

66. Ibid., 103.

67. Ibid., 35.

68. Gustafson, "The Place of Scripture," 45.

— 3 —

"MALE AND FEMALE":
Sexual Differentiation
in Genesis

Important resources for the Christian understanding of man, woman, and sexuality are the stories of God's creation of humanity in Genesis 1—3. These imaginative portrayals of the fundamental natures and relations of humanity and God, man and woman, and good and evil have been interpreted, reinterpreted, and often misinterpreted throughout Judeo-Christian tradition. Jesus himself is presented in the Gospels as invoking the creation in support of the fidelity marriage requires (Mark 10:1–2; Matt. 19:1–2). Some epistles recall Eve's creation (1 Cor. 11:7–9, 12) or sin (1 Tim. 2: 11–15) in defining the role of woman. Important patristic, medieval, and Reformation authors draw on Genesis in shaping the views of sexuality and sexual hierarchy that prevailed in much of Christian history. Biblical scholars, theologians, and ethicists today return to these powerful and illuminating texts to seek the renewal, transformation, or even rejection of some past and present images. Still, they are concerned to remain faithful to the genesis and thrust of that religious world view which they take in its essential respects to be normative. I will argue that the stories of creation and fall in Genesis exclude rather than encourage a hierarchical view of the sexes. They depict as normative the equal partnership of women and men in caring for the creation, in procreating their own kind, and in providing one another with companionship.

CREATION IN GENESIS

The primeval history in the Bible's first book is designed to show the acts and purposes of Yahweh; it reveals the God of Israel as the

God of nature and history. Within this history are included two distinct accounts of the creation of the human race. The one that appears first, by the Priestly author, dates from the sixth century B.C., around the time of the fall of the nation and exile. It tells of the creation of humanity in God's image and as simultaneously male and female (Gen. 1:26–28). The second, by the Yahwist, is chronologically earlier, dating from the time of the monarchy in the tenth century B.C. It describes the creation of male and female successively, with "man" (*'ādām*) being formed of "dust from the ground" (*hā-'adāmâ*) by the Lord, who then casts him into a deep sleep and takes the woman (*'iššâ*) from his rib. Man (*'îš*) and woman (*'iššâ*) become "one flesh" (Gen. 2:4–25). The two then disobediently eat of the fruit of the tree that the serpent has promised will make them wise, and are sent forth by God from the garden (Genesis 3). Both creation accounts affirm that God's work, including the creation of humanity, is good and harmonious. The one written from a perspective of historical disaster and despair describes humanity as the bearer of God's image and likeness. Yet even the Yahwist, writing from the vantage point of prosperity, recalls that humanity is not divine, but made by God from the earth. Although God transcends sexuality and is neither male nor female, the distinction of the sexes is necessary to complete mankind, and is the precondition for the procreative power that corresponds to the divine command to multiply. Our discussion of Genesis 1 will allow us to pose the question of the significance of the divine image and its relation to sexual differentiation and to the equality of the sexes. Genesis 2 will force us to ask whether sequential creation implies hierarchy, a problem the judgments that fall on the man and the woman in Genesis 3 can illumine.

Genesis 1

In a recent essay on the creation account in the first chapter of Genesis,[1] Phyllis A. Bird, an Old Testament scholar, observes not only that the text's reference to the divine image in conjunction with the male and female has been a continuing source of fascination for theologians as well as for interpreters, but also that the former have pursued their inquiries with too great a degree of independence from the latter. She criticizes dogmatic constructions, whether traditional or feminist, that are framed in terms of concerns, questions, and assumptions foreign to and uncritically imposed upon the text. Too often, "approval of the theological construction is taken as validation of the exegesis."[2] The historical and constructive tasks must be related—but distinguished in order to be related.

Few ethicists, however, possess the tools that would enable original investigation of what a given text meant to its author(s) or editor(s). The ethicist must decide not only the degree to which what the Bible means depends on or is derived from what it originally meant; but also by which criteria one exegetical account of the original meaning is to be preferred over another. The Christian ethicist who attends seriously to the investigations of biblical scholars will do well to avoid excessive dependence on a particular view or consensus which may later be upset by the historical, descriptive inquiries of biblical scholars. Thus I shall rely for the most part on reasonable scholarly consensus about the historical meanings of texts. At no point will I presume to propose novel interpretation, though I may make evaluative judgments about the implications of accepted interpretation for ongoing theological reflection by measuring the consistency of apparently original textual meanings with relevant premises of Christian ethics confirmed by or derived from other sources. This is one way in which the competence of the theologian can complement that of the interpreter.[3] In the present discussion of the Genesis creation stories, the point of focus will be sexual differentiation and the relationship of equality or inequality between the sexes. In chapter 5 I will examine the relevance of some empirical research on gender differentiation both to the images of Genesis and to some New Testament views of woman.

> Then God said, "Let us make man ['ādām] in our image, after our likeness; and let them have dominion. . . ." So God created man ['ādām] in his own image, in the image of God he created him; male and female he created them. And God blessed them, and God said to them, "Be fruitful and multiply. . . ." (Gen. 1:26–28)

This text juxtaposes the creation of humanity ('ādām) in God's image with its creation as male and female. What conclusions legitimately may be drawn from this? The conclusion that male and female are equally in God's image, and in fact together and in re-

lationship as complementary forms of humanity constitute humanity's likeness to God, is attractive from the viewpoint of normative
ethics. This is particularly so when feminist or egalitarian concerns
are on the agenda. Such a reading would support a communitarian
view of male and female, and of humanity as mirroring in its sociality
the Trinitarian relationships. Such conclusions about the relation of
the sexes may be theologically and ethically appropriate if evaluated
on the basis of the combined and complementary reference points
of Christian ethics (Scripture, tradition, philosophical or "normative" accounts, and factual or "descriptive" accounts of the human).
But to what degree or in what way are they warranted by the text
considered for the moment independently?

Here it is necessary to take seriously the interpreter's insistence
that the verses alluding to image of God and to male and female be
read in a larger context of at least the Priestly (P) creation narrative.
For example, Bird argues persuasively that P is interested in portraying all creation as dependent on God and ordered by God. The
author explicitly attends to the means by which each creature shall
be sustained, for example, by specifying that vegetation bears seeds
(Gen. 1:20–21, 24). To *'ādām*, as to the other forms of life, is addressed the blessing of increase: "Be fruitful and multiply" (Gen.
1:28). Human sexual differentiation, the presupposition of this command, must be specified rather than assumed, as it is for the animals,
precisely because of the immediately preceding statement that humanity is made in the image of the divinity, who transcends sexuality. Thus the theme of sexual complementarity does not expand
upon that of image, but is distinct from it. It represents the theme
of the sustainability of nature, not that of position and dominion
within the created order. Not only is it the case that the Priestly
author construes no special correspondence between the sexes and
the nature of God, but Gen. 1:27 does not contradict this view,
supported by the male genealogies in the Priestly author's account
(e.g., in Genesis 5 and 12), that men have a special role in history
and that women appear on the scene primarily to fulfill the biological
role of reproduction.[4]

Already I have alluded to the distinction that must exist between
the descriptive and constructive phases of biblical hermeneutics, a
distinction affirmed by Bird, who has given us a hypothesis about

how the original meaning of Genesis 1 might best be described. In chapter 2, I argued that while the meaning that a text probably had for the community that produced it is important for later normative interpretation, the former alone does not determine the latter. Sandra Schneiders warns against exclusive focus on "the literal sense" of a text.[5] The contemporary historical-critical methods which allow increasingly greater recovery of this meaning have come to dominate biblical scholarship, but these methods in themselves do not constitute a model for the normative function of the materials to which they are applied. Like Thomas Ogletree, Schneiders suggests that the meaning of a text once written is no longer limited to that which it had for its original audience, but is inclusive of those that it takes on for subsequent audiences. The interpreter of the biblical text in effect enters into a "dialogue" with it on the basis of a common religious tradition, even though the questions and concerns of the ancient author may not be identical to those brought to the text today.

Schneiders also notes that contemporary interpretations of the text must in some sense be "controlled by the text."[6] In other words, the written text provides a point of contact between the original and subsequent meanings, which ought not in essence to be at odds with one another. As we have seen, the difficult questions for the theologian as interpreter and interpreter as theologian will be how to determine what "faithfulness to a text" means and what are the criteria of a text's "controlling" meaning.

One proposed avenue of appropriation of biblical texts for normative theology and ethics is that of literary criticism. By examining the internal structure and language of a text, the interpreter allows the text to communicate in a relatively independent manner. Of course, historical-critical methods will also be employed, for example, in the determination of the possible senses in which a word included in the text might be used. Phyllis Trible offers us an example of literary analysis of Gen. 1:27 when she argues that the verse is an instance of nuanced and connotative poetic language.[7] Chiasmus and parallel structures within the verse support a correspondence of "image of God" and "male and female," from which Trible concludes that humankind is two sexually different creatures who are equal in likeness to God, power over the earth, and authority in regard to one another.

Trible's hermeneutic of the text is not tied to a claim that the significance that she attributes to it is identical to that with which it was invested by the Priestly writer. If an analysis such as that of Bird's is correct, the theme of male-female equality would have been foreign and probably objectionable to the Priestly author and to the religious community whose faith was expressed. Yet in favor of Trible's interpretation it can be urged that the text itself connotes certain meanings that become apparent on the basis of a subsequent community's attempts to apply insights of a faith tradition that also includes the community of authorship. Continuity with the essential core of that same faith tradition is enabled if not infallibly guaranteed, first, by reference to the internal meaning of the shared text; and, second, by reference to the mutually correcting sources of the tradition's normative constructions. Although what the Bible "meant" is not absolutely authoritative for the ongoing community of interpretation, neither is what the Bible "means" absolutely open.

It also must be recognized that methods purported to reveal the author's "original intention" and those used to define the meaning of the text "in itself" cannot be distinguished radically, nor can their object. We might, for example, consider that a scholar like Bird analyzes the *structure* of a text to reveal something about the explicit and *implicit* purposes of its composer. Bird's argument about the fertility theme of Genesis 1 includes references to textual parallels to the blessing of increase directed to humanity, and comments on the structure of "announcement" and "execution report" which frame the account of humanity's creation. Although Trible does not claim that her conclusions about male and female and the image of God would be shared by the Priestly writer, we cannot exclude the possibility, even likelihood, that the structure of the writer's poetry, from which the conclusions of the literary critic are drawn, emerges from fundamental, if inchoate, insights of the Priestly author's community into the nature of humanity and its standing before God.

Thus it is necessary to qualify any interpretation theory that claims to read the meaning of a text simply as a literary unity taken on its own terms. What the text means to the ongoing community of the church has a necessary connection with what it meant to the

community that produced it. The present shape and internal coherence of a text, which is the object of literary analysis, is partly
contingent on the function and use it had for its original author and
his particular audience. To understand what this function must have
been is also to gain insight into the meaning the text bears in the
present, because it enables us to supply connecting links between
function, structure, and "message." We increase our appreciation
of a text's significance by classifying it into a literary genre, at which
we arrive partly by a study of structure and partly by historical
research which illumines what the social context might have been
for the construction of a text with that structure. Thus the meaning
communicated by the text is dependent on structure and language
that emerges from a life situation that made that structure appropriate for the expression of an "original" meaning. "Meaning for us"
has an indispensable chain of connection to "meaning for them."

For instance, one of the continuing meanings that Bird enables
us to draw out of the Priestly creation account is the linking of gender
difference and sex with procreation, and procreation with obedience
to God's intention for the preservation of the created orders.[8] The
repetitive structure of announcement and performance report, and
the parallel provisions for the preservation of each kind of creature,
to which Bird refers in construing the original meaning of the text,
are seen simultaneously to facilitate ritual repetition and to support
the function of the text as a "creation hymn" by giving a structural
and poetic impression of God's ordering of what he has made.[9]

We will notice a similar connection of function, structure, and
meaning in the Yahwist account (Genesis 2), which concerns the
creation of humanity rather than of the universe. It originally cir-
culated as a popular tradition answering questions about "why
things are the way they are" (childbirth, toil, the rule of men).[10]
The structure of Genesis 3, for example, is constituted by parallel
judgments which not only place man and woman equally under the
burden of sin, but also would have facilitated storytelling, and which
draw the contemporary eye to the similarities and differences between the sinners and their punishments. The Yahwist has incorporated the ancient etiological story into Israel's covenant faith in
the sovereign God and its recognition of sin as rebellion. Like the
Priestly author, the Yahwist shows the work and purposes of God

in history, and expresses the view of continuing importance that the actual situation of men and women is the result of sin and a distortion of the will of the Creator.

The end result of our analysis of Gen. 1:26–28 is that it yields certain implications for a positive theology and ethics of sexuality. Sexual difference and relationship are intrinsically human, good, and fruitful. Normative as against nonnormative meanings of the text can be determined only within the hermeneutical circle of the mutually defining boundaries of the Christian self-understanding. The biblical communities ground the tradition that interprets the Bible (whose canonical authority consists in the sum effect of mutually defining texts and books). Yet the shape of the interpreting community is corrected not only by the Scriptures but also by ideal conceptions of the human and the testing of those against the human reality.

In the light of complementary biblical and nonbiblical criteria, some possible implications of the text will be rejected. For example, woman is not to be defined primarily in terms of her procreative role. Such an understanding would be inconsistent with the perspective that the canon itself provides on the text. The inclusion of all humans in the "image of God" and a model of partnership in Genesis 2 are to be found. Recourse may also be had to nonbiblical complementary sources. Although the Judeo-Christian tradition, philosophical definitions of what humanity is essentially, and even empirical research, have certainly given rise to sexist interpretations of woman, I think a reasonable argument can be made on the basis of these same sources that the humanity of woman entails for her more than a procreative role vis-à-vis the race.

The *positive* implications of Genesis 1, to summarize, are at least fourfold. First, with the evident understanding of the original author, we can consistently affirm that sexual differentiation and cooperation are linked to procreation. Maleness and femaleness have as a purpose the human response to the Lord's "Be fruitful." This does not, however, entail necessarily the conclusion that all male-female relations, all sexual acts, or all marital partnerships exist for the sole or even inalienable purpose of procreation. Second, we can affirm normatively some perspectives on the place of individual within community that are congenial to the viewpoint of the Priestly author. Contrary to modern liberalism, the Priestly author places the man-woman relation in the context of the welfare of the creation, rather than of interpersonal communion. Even their sexual coming together is in fulfillment of their responsibility to propagate the inclusive community of their species, and so to support the maintenance of the created orders. Male and female relations, it can be said, find definition and meaning in "the common good."

Interpretation theory, not to mention the fairly constant practice of the faith tradition, also legitimates the project of articulating theological conclusions that depart from the text's original meaning but which can be construed as developments of the text. Third, the structure of the text encourages us to associate the image of God with both male and female and to view them as equal in dignity and authority. Fourth, and finally, the text also can be aligned with the insight that the communal nature of humanity as male and female, already acknowledged by the Priestly author as definitive of the race, and in fact of sexuality itself as the differentiation and union of male and female, is a mirror of the divinity, whom the text also represents as making plural self-references ("Let us make man [*'ādām*] in our image, after our likeness," Gen. 1:27). This is not to say of course that the author of the text intended any Trinitarian doctrine of God.

Genesis 2

The creation narrative of the Yahwist in Genesis 2 raises parallel hermeneutical issues. It expands the meaning of Genesis 1 insofar as sexuality is construed in terms of companionship, commitment, and social cooperation as well as of biological complementarity for procreation. A key question for ethics posed by Genesis 2 is whether the woman's being taken from the man's rib and designated his "helper" entails a normatively hierarchical view of male and female relationships.

One point of possible dispute in regard to this text is the nature of the creature from which the woman is taken. Trible, again using the tools of the literary critic, points to the similarity between the Hebrew words for "man" (*'ādām*) and "the earth" (*hā-'adāmâ*), from which the man was made, and suggests that "earth creature" translates *'ādām* better than "man." She concludes from this that Genesis 2 portrays an initial creation of a sexually undifferentiated (not androgynous) being, whom God differentiates by a subsequent act into male ('*iš*) and female ('*iššâ*).[11] On Trible's reading, the man does not exist before the woman. Both come into existence simultaneously; it is the creation of humanity and sexuality, not of male and female, that is successive.

While this interpretation has the advantage, considered from the perspective of normative ethics, of supporting the equality of male and female, it seems to have the disadvantage of suggesting that humanity is not intrinsically sexual, a view I take to be at odds with the anthropologies both of the biblical author and of the Christian tradition. If we allow that the text, as well as what its author explicitly intended to the extent that that can be recovered, stands to be modified in a subsequent hermeneutics of appropriation, using sources beyond Scripture, then it becomes proportionately less important to deny that aspects of the account represent simply the patriarchy of tenth-century Israel. The story is told from the man's point of view, and it is taken for granted that the creation of the female is secondary to that of the male.[12]

The account itself, however, provides other clues to the modification of its own androcentric elements, and a challenge to the idea that there existed a complete human being before the creation of the woman, and a superior one after it. God sizes up the situation of the original solitariness of '*ādām* with the statement, "It is not good" (Gen. 2:18), then proposes to make a "helper" (Gen. 2:18). Although that word in English carries connotations of subordination, its Hebrew original ('*ēzer*) is never used elsewhere in the Scriptures to designate an inferior. In fact, it sometimes refers to God as the savior of Israel.[13] Further, the creation of both man and woman are preceded by God's reflection and involve direct divine action, the mysterious nature of which is connoted by the "deep sleep" which God causes to fall upon '*ādām* (Gen. 2:21). The origin of the reference to the "rib" as the source of the woman is unclear, but its effect in the story is to indicate the unity of nature of male and female and the superiority of the latter to the animals which God has already tried and found wanting as companions for the man. That the term suggests the secondary nature of the woman in relation to the man should be rejected. For one, the man is made from "dust," but is not for that reason inferior to it, since it is simply the raw material upon which God acts. For another, the sequence of creation after the '*ādām*, from the garden to the animals to the woman, has progressed from lower to higher, a detail that seems to favor the superiority of the final sort of human being that God has made! We also find that the "one flesh" unity of male and female is consolidated by the act of the husband, who leaves family and "cleaves to" his wife (Gen. 2:24). This is a historically remarkable stipulation because it was the woman who was assimilated by the man's family in Israelite society.[14]

According to Genesis 1 and 2, then, humanity, the two sexes, and sexuality are created good and are designed for a harmonious and productive existence. Genesis 3 narrates the use of human freedom to propel the sexes, and with them the creation, down a path of disruption, alienation, and suffering.

The judgments that follow God's discovery of the pair's disobedience describe its personal, social, and cosmic effects. The woman is to bear children, and the man to cultivate the earth, in pain (Gen. 3:16–19), until they return to dust. The wife's "desire" for her husband will be reciprocated by his "rule over" her (Gen. 3:16). It is only after their fall from original harmony that the man names the woman "Eve," reducing her to the status of the animals he named in Genesis 2 (Gen. 3:19–20). The partnership of the creation is transmuted into disorder and suffering, of which the historical supremacy of the male and the definition of one sex by procreative and domestic roles, and the other by economic and productive ones, will be a manifestation. The Lord's discourse describes an effect of sin on the created order rather than prescribing that order's intrinsic design.[15] The hierarchy of the sexes is the consequence and perpetuation of sin, corrupting the dominator as well as the dominated. It is ironically appropriate that the more passive sinner, the man, who took and ate, now is condemned to the exertion of laboring to wrest human sustenance from a resistant environment; the more active sinner, the woman, who debated with the serpent and led her husband, is condemned not only to subordination to the man, but also to helpless submission to the inexorable pain of childbirth. But what is the sum effect of the judgment? It is to condemn equally pride as active self-assertion and pride as passive complacency. Hope and God's continuing care for the con-

victed creatures is communicated in a final mitigating reference to
their now-shameful nakedness: "And the Lord God made for
Adam and for his wife garments of skins, and clothed them" (Gen.
3:21).[16]

In reviewing the implications of the first three chapters of Genesis
for a normative Christian understanding of the relation between the
sexes, we find that supremacy and subordination, as distinct from
difference and cooperation, are not part of the original creation but
of the condition of sin. God's creation of humanity in the divine
image, as male and female, and as companions who become "one
flesh," functions as a standard by which to evaluate and criticize
the male and female dialogue and struggle in history. We see that
woman and man are ordained *normatively* to community. Their society is ordered by their commanded roles of dominion of other creatures and propagation of their own species. Their psycho-social partnership finds significance in the context of these divine mandates.
In the fulfillment of the resulting obligations, man and woman have
equal responsibility and dignity.[17]

NOTES

1. Phyllis A. Bird, "'Male and Female He Created Them': Gen. 1:27b in
the Context of the Priestly Account of Creation," *Harvard Theological Review*
74/2 (1981): 129–59.

2. Ibid., 132.

3. James M. Gustafson has argued that any prescriptive sexual ethics (and,
by extension, any ethics of relationships between the sexes) must attend to
three "fundamental bases." These are human nature, both biological and "personal"; the reality of moral and religious evil or sin; and "the social character
of human experience" ("Nature, Sin, and Covenant: Three Bases for Sexual
Ethics," *Perspectives in Biology and Medicine* [Spring 1981]: 483–97). Biblical accounts provide one sort of material with which to establish these bases; these
accounts must be complemented by philosophical, traditional, and empirical
sources.

4. Bird, "'Male and Female,'" 156. Joseph Jensen also agrees that Genesis
1 highlights procreation, while Genesis 2 contributes the theme of companionship, making the texts complementary ("Human Sexuality in the Scriptures," *Human Sexuality and Personhood: Proceedings of the Workshop for the Hierarchies of the United States and Canada Sponsored by the Pope John Center through a
Grant from the Knights of Columbus* (St. Louis: Pope John Center, 1981), 15–16.

5. Sandra M. Schneiders, "From Exegesis to Hermeneutics: The Problem of the Contemporary Meaning of Scripture," *Horizons* 8/1 (1981): 30.

6. Ibid., 34.

7. Phyllis Trible, *God and the Rhetoric of Sexuality*, Overtures to Biblical Theology 2 (Philadelphia: Fortress Press, 1978), 15–21.

8. Bernhard Anderson is commenting on the structure that enhances that meaning when he notes that the "stately rhythms and sonorous refrains" of the Priestly narrative "reflect years of usage in the Temple, where it was solemnly recited and gradually assumed its present form of liturgical prose" (*Understanding the Old Testament* [Englewood Cliffs, N.J.: Prentice-Hall, 1957], 426).

9. A like effect is created by the repeated statement, "God saw that it was good," which functions as a liturgical or mnemonic device. Eugene H. Maly, "Genesis," *Jerome Biblical Commentary*, ed. Raymond E. Brown, Joseph A. Fitzmyer, Roland E. Murphy (Englewood Cliffs, N.J.: Prentice-Hall, 1968), 10.

10. Anderson, *Understanding the Old Testament*, 211; Gerhard von Rad, *Old Testament Theology* (New York: Harper & Row; Edinburgh: Oliver and Boyd, 1962), 1:150.

11. While *'ādām* is a term that can be used either to designate the species or an individual man, or to mean a proper name, the Hebrew word that can be used *only* for a single male (*'îš*) is not used until the creation of the woman, to whom reference is made by the corollary Hebrew term for a single female (*'iššâ*). Against Trible's thesis, however, stands the fact that *'ādām* continues to be used (along with *'îš*) in reference to the male after the creation of the woman.

12. Bird, "Images of Women in the Old Testament"; Paul K. Jewett, *Man as Male and Female* (Grand Rapids: Wm. B. Eerdmans, 1975), 86–94. Although women shared in the covenant relationship, the social and religious institutions of Israelite society were undeniably patriarchal.

13. Trible, *God and the Rhetoric of Sexuality*, 90; Jewett, *Man as Male and Female*, 124.

14. Jewett, *Man as Male and Female*, 124–28. Cf. Trible, *God and the Rhetoric of Sexuality*, 96. Jewett also points out that it is important to maintain a distinction between the creation of the woman in 2:18–23 and marriage in 2:24. The second presupposes the first, but they are not the same. In the Hebrew Bible as a whole, the male-female distinction came to be understood almost entirely in terms of the marriage relation, possibly because of the covenant promise to "Abraham's seed" (pp. 120–21).

15. See Bruce Vawter, *A Path through Genesis* (New York and London: Sheed & Ward, 1956), 59, 69.

16. Cf. Trible, *God and the Rhetoric of Sexuality*, 134. My discussion of the passive and active sinners is indebted to the comments of Cheryl Exum. See also the observations of Theodore Mackin, *What is Marriage?* (New York: Paulist Press, 1982), 47.

17. In *God and the Rhetoric of Sexuality*, Trible includes a compelling discussion of the portrayal of the sexes and sexuality in the Song of Songs as a text complementary to Genesis. The interaction of man and woman in love, sex, and work is portrayed there in freedom from sex role stereotypes (pp. 144–65). An ethicist who also has linked the ideal pictures of Genesis and of the Song is James Nelson, *Between Two Gardens: Reflections on Sexuality and Religious Experience* (New York: Pilgrim Press, 1983), esp. chap. 1.

—— 4 ——

NEW TESTAMENT PERSPECTIVES on Community, Sex, and the Sexes

The focus of this chapter on the New Testament resources for a Christian ethics of sexuality will be primarily the Pauline letters (especially 1 Corinthians), and secondarily the New Testament divorce texts. I might justify my choice of Paul among other biblical authors by pointing out that he mentions sexual morality more frequently than any other, though still with relative infrequency, and that 1 Corinthians 7 contains the only extended discussion of sexual relationships in the entire New Testament. All this has been observed before, and would be true. But my more essential motive is the import for Christian ethics of Paul's locating all particular moral activity in the context of communal life. In the area of sexuality in particular, Christian ethics has been characterized by an unfortunate, and unbiblical, "bottom line" mentality: precisely which acts are permissible for whom, and under what circumstances? Biblical authors, to the contrary, mention moral acts only in connection with the faith orientation that they express, and never approach sexual conduct as a realm preeminently definitive of one's standing before God. Paul's approach to sex, celibacy, and marriage is instructive, because he sees them as manifestations of the sort of life a religious community and its members have achieved.

Paul relates morality to the body of Christ as a present reality made possible by the Spirit and oriented by its hope for the return of the Lord. The convert who lives in the Spirit also acts in a way that "builds up" the community (e.g., 1 Cor. 14:3, 12; 1 Thess. 5:11; Col. 2:6–7); one's membership in the community and one's personal conduct are all of a piece with one's faith in the gospel.[1] The communal reference of the concrete advice given by Paul, including that on sex, celibacy, marriage, and divorce, is heightened when taken together with the divorce texts in Matthew, Mark, and Luke, in which a teaching of Jesus is adapted variously.

My decision that the theme of community, and the biblical texts that substantiate it, are normative for Christian ethics, is warranted by the biblical source of ethics, and also supported by nonbiblical sources. I think it hardly needs to be argued that communal images such as "covenant people," "people of God," and "kingdom of God" characterize both the Old and New Testaments. Thus particular texts or books articulating this theme, and a normative ethics based on them, would at least in that respect express a "biblical" point of view. In addition, human sociality, and the importance for normative ethics of recognizing human interrelationship as a criterion of genuinely human existence, is borne out by other reference points. We might rely on philosophical views of the person's essential and positive relation to others and to the common good, or on descriptive accounts of actual societies as the condition of possibility of the development of individuality. The Christian tradition too emphasizes the fundamental link of the individual to church and to civil society. Today in particular the communal nature of the person and of moral agency needs to be stressed over against some expressions of Western liberal democracy and individualism. In fact, our sensitivity to biblical support for the value and normative status of community may be heightened by our reaction against the extremes of liberalism, just as liberalism itself resisted the overriding of the individual's interests by those of society or state. This is again evidence of the point that culture and Bible form a dialectic of presupposition and critique.[2]

Another reason for my interest in Paul as a focus of analysis is that he often is interpreted not only as pronouncing specific and negative moral rules which have the weight of "Scripture," but also as taking an unappreciative view of sex, marriage, and women in general. I am prepared to argue that Paul's views of sex, celibacy, and marriage make more sense, and come more into line with other biblical views of sex, if we consider them in relation to a communal criterion of morality, and if we set them against the background of an imminent eschatology. As will become apparent, it is not only specific evaluations (e.g., of celibacy and marriage) that must meet the communal criterion; *reinterpretation* of authoritative norms already articulated is carried out by this criterion. The divorce texts will be used to demonstrate this point. It is in view of changing community circumstances that the biblical authors themselves appropriate differently the apparently original absolute prohibition of divorce by Jesus.

It is striking that we find not only in Paul, but in the whole New Testament, a relative lack of emphasis on specific moral judgments and universal moral rules, as well as on sex generally as an area of special ethical interest. As J. L. Houlden has observed in commenting on the place of ethics in the New Testament, conduct and virtue are commended there not for their own sakes, but because "they are characteristics of God or of Jesus, and are therefore to be imitated as part of a life of discipleship" (cf. 1 Cor. 11:1, "Be imitators of me as I am of Christ"). Further, moral principles, for example, those relating to sexual activity, are not grounded as frequently in the actual conduct of Jesus as they are in the pattern of his redeeming work (e.g., see the deutero-Pauline modeling in Ephesians 5 of the husband-wife relationship on the relation between Christ and his church).[3] Another important element in the moral perspectives of the New Testament is the eschatological horizon of community formation.[4] As we shall see, the shifting of this horizon for succeeding generations of Christians may have significant implications for some of Paul's particular evaluations.

The communal criterion of the moral life that Paul's perspective on membership in the body of Christ offers is consistent with the normative view of sexuality which can be based upon Genesis 1—3. These Genesis chapters reveal and affirm the communal significance of sexual differentiation, complementarity, and partnership. Sexuality is portrayed there as the precondition of humanity's support of the order of creation through the procreation of the species, and also as the sine qua non of the partnership of man and woman in fulfilling the Lord God's commands.

Most of the hermeneutical and methodological issues that arose in regard to the Genesis creation accounts will continue to be crucial for our examination of New Testament sources. I will rely on some

principles already adduced: (1) The Bible is one source among others, but it is the fundamental source for Christian theological ethics.
(2) It is possible to distinguish what the Bible *meant* to its original
author(s) and to its original audience from what it *means* for the
ongoing church, though the two cannot be disconnected. (3) There
may be a normative meaning of a text, common at some level both
to what was understood by it originally and to its normative function
in the ongoing community, which can be distinguished from elements that are less central, or more conditioned culturally—the
"ethos" of the writer.[5] (4) There exists an inescapable and large
hermeneutical circle in which the Christian ethicist's task of biblical
reappropriation must proceed. The ethicist uses biblical criteria to
evaluate the moral decisions, acts, principles, and habits found in
his or her culture, but relies on culturally informed insights from
philosophy, science, and the Christian tradition itself to select what
is "essential" and "authoritative" in the biblical canon.

SEXUALITY AND COMMUNITY
IN 1 CORINTHIANS

The First Letter to the Corinthians is occasioned by reports to
Paul of disturbing attempts by Corinthian converts to import into
Christianity some mystical, enthusiastic, or ascetic strains of current
philosophy. Some apparently thought that the kingdom could be
realized perfectly in the lives of a few individuals or groups. This
influenced them toward factiousness and elitism (1 Cor. 1:10–11;
11:18–22), and had resulted, for example, in disputes over the Christian's freedom to eat idol offerings (1 Corinthians 8), over which
gifts of the Spirit were more valuable and prestigious (1 Corinthians
12—14), and in aberrant views of sexual activity. Some may have
maintained that sex should be excluded for all Christians, or that
the way the Christian uses sex is irrelevant to his or her membership
in the community of faith (cf. 1 Cor. 7:1–2). Paul responds to these
controversies by reminding church members of their common life
in the Spirit, and their equality in Christ's body; and by instructing
(*paraklēsis*) them to live and act in a manner that serves the community—in short, to "strive to excel in building the church" (1 Cor.
14:12).

The New Testament's longest discourse on sexual activity and the states in which it is or is not carried out occurs in the middle of this discussion of community. Paul clearly states that celibacy is to be preferred to marriage, and certainly to sexual activity outside of marriage, but celibacy is not made into a general rule of Christian living (1 Cor. 7:6–7, 38).[6] In fact, Paul counsels everyone, married or unmarried, slave or free, circumcised or uncircumcised, to remain "in whatever state each was called" (1 Cor. 7:24; cf. 7:17–24), and to concentrate singleheartedly on serving the Lord. All temporal states and the concerns that bind us to the world are relativized by the coming of the kingdom.

Paul's attitudes toward sex and marriage are framed in 1 Corinthians 7 not only by his solicitousness for the body of Christ but also by the urgent expectation of the first-generation Christians that the Parousia would arrive in their own lifetimes. Paul warns of "the impending distress" (1 Cor. 7:26), and observes that "the form of this world is passing away" (7:31). He seeks to lead his audience in ways of living which will "spare" them "worldly troubles" (7:28). From what Paul has seen of life, and inferred of wedded couples, he suspects that "the married man is anxious about worldly affairs, how to please his wife" (7:33), while the wife is anxious about "how to please her husband," and so too her "interests are divided" (7:34). Paul, on the other hand, wants only "to secure your undivided devotion to the Lord" (7:35).

Whether Paul's qualms are justified or not, the married may be in a better position than he to tell. Paul half concedes as much in his concluding advice to the widow to avoid remarriage, when he allows that his estimate that her happiness will be greater if she is not a wife is a matter of "judgment," not doctrine. He supports his own opinion rather tentatively for one usually so assured: "And I think that I have the Spirit of God" (7:40; cf. 7:25, where Paul expresses his "opinion" on the unmarried in general).

It is arguable that Paul thinks of marriage positively only in regard to the legitimation of the satisfaction of sexual desire (7:2, 36). As far as this purpose is concerned, however, husband and wife have equal rights (7:3–4). But he certainly develops no view of the married state as enabling the joint service of man and woman to community, even though such a view would not be inconsistent with the partnership established in Genesis.[7] Paul does not speak specifically even of procreation as a purpose of marriage, which is not surprising in view of his anticipation that his generation of Christians is to be the last. It is only in the immediate future that Paul can contemplate any direct contribution of marital fidelity to the communal up-building which he repeatedly mentions. In discussing separation of married couples, Paul remarks that children of a Christian and a pagan spouse, as well as the unbelieving husband or wife, can be "consecrated" through the faithfulness of the Christian (7:14–16). In general, however, Paul sees, not marriage alone, but also all preoccupation with one's social state in life, as a distraction and a hindrance to communal membership.

The communal context of sexual ethics is also disclosed in the much-cited and controverted Pauline references to *porneia*, or "sexual immorality" (e.g., Gal. 5:19; Rom. 1:24; 1 Thess. 4:3–5; Col. 3:5; 1 Cor. 5:9–10, 6:9–10; 7:2). *Porneia* can be translated variously as "prostitution," "fornication," "adultery," and "unchastity" or "impurity."[8] (The verb *porneuō* also occurs, e.g., 1 Cor. 6:18; 10:8; cf. Rev. 2:14, 20 in connection with idol worship.) The earliest of Paul's letters, 1 Thessalonians, is typical in that it presents sexual sin and self-control in the context of "how you ought to live and to please God" (1 Thess. 4:1) and of "love of the brethren" and "wrong" to one's brother (4:9,6). Clearly the language marks the train of thought as a man's point of view, and possibly even indicates that the author sees sexual transgression involving a woman as primarily an injustice to the man who has charge of her. Here, however, *porneia* (3:3) defines what kind of activity is or is not a fulfillment of Paul's earlier exhortation "to lead a life worthy of God, who calls you into his own kingdom and glory" (2:12), and "who gives his Holy Spirit to you" (4:8). Paul not only excludes certain behavior, but also enjoins behavior exhibiting diligence, peaceableness, patience, generosity, piety, and gratitude (4:10–12; 5:12–22), because it enables the converts to "encourage one another and build one another up" (5:11).

Paul is not concerned so much with the avoidance of vice, much less with the precise stipulation of the kinds of sexual acts in which vice consists, as he is with portraying for the young churches the sort of communities they must be if they are truly to live in the Spirit as members of one body. All sorts of moral perversions result from any perversion of the fundamental relationship between creature and Creator (Rom. 1:18–32). When he is setting aside the kinds of people who will not inherit the kingdom, Paul draws the specifics from lists of vices which would have been familiar to his audience because of their currency in contemporary Jewish missionary preaching. To the new Christians, his message is simply that they exist in categories such as these no longer, for they already have been justified and sanctified in the Lord Jesus Christ and the Spirit of God (1 Cor. 6:9–13). In the body of Christ, conformity to God's will in love and obedience will so prevail that the condemnation and exclusion of sin need not be at issue (1 Corinthians 13).

In summary, we can say that Paul's discussion of sexual acts and relations in 1 Corinthians 7 is controlled by two concerns. One is his primary intention to hold up incorporation in and service to the body of Christ as the source and norm of Christian living; the other is the peculiar eschatological framework within which the requisites of membership in Christ are elaborated.

ESCHATOLOGY AND
SEXUAL ETHICS

Pheme Perkins has made available for the ethicist some of the results of recent biblical criticism and exegesis. She comments that it is not the command to love itself that radically marks the ethical content of the gospel, but "the expectation that the final judgment is near."[9] This leads the New Testament authors to focus on preparation in the renewed faith community for the immediate return of the Lord, rather than on the long-term shape of the community or on the involvement of the church in rectifying social violations of justice. At the same time, however, the eschatological vision of the community does not center exclusively on the future: "They saw, in the emergence of a new people of God based on the salvation brought in Jesus, the beginning and sign of the new age, which they expected to come with the judgment."[10] The New Testament eschatological expectation is not only hoped for, but also realized in the present. God's rule is not only future; it is near and "at hand."[11]

Writing in the third decade after the death of Jesus, Paul certainly anticipates that the Lord will return soon, even in Paul's own lifetime. Thus the theme of future expectation is prominent in his preaching and exhortations to the communities he has founded. This is quite obvious in the discourse on marriage and celibacy of 1 Corinthians 7. At the same time, Paul does recognize that the kingdom already is accessible wherever the community lives in the Spirit. Appreciation of the opportunity to realize the kingdom in the present increases in proportion to the delay of the *parousia*.[12] Both future and present elements, however, always have been normative for the Christian preaching of the kingdom of God.

Paul's proclamation in Galatians that those who have been baptized into Christ are "all one," so that "there is neither slave nor free, there is neither male nor female . . ." (3:28; cf. 1 Cor. 7:13), can be understood as a recognition of the present reality of the kingdom, even though the social institutions and structures in and through which it is embodied are provisional. (Paul does not challenge the historical existence of the institutionalized divisions that are transcended in Christ.) This note of realized eschatology also echoes in some of Paul's comments on sexual activity, insofar as he relates the present actions of the Christian to actual existence in Christ's body. The body of Christ is a living reality, and all activity in which a Christian engages has a very direct effect upon it. Thus Paul condemns so vehemently the sacrilegious act of a Christian joining with a prostitute (1 Cor. 6:15–20). The comparison of husband and wife to Christ and church in Eph. 5:25 also reflects the possibility that relationships that characterize the kingdom can be realized concretely in the lives of Christians.

As Houlden remarks, the pastoral epistles, written by second-generation followers of Paul, are evidence that reflection on the moral life becomes more important in the community as the expected imminence of the end time declines.[13] Paul is interested in the solidarity of the body of Christ, but not so much in specific moral problems as in the type of religious existence of which they are the manifestation. This is why he is liable to adopt "conventional" views on particulars, for instance, lists of vices or standards of domestic and ecclesiastical order.[14] Even though he makes statements about marriage and celibacy, his attention really is not focused on the institution of marriage, the day-to-day and long-term relations of spouses or family members.

It may be this difference in the perception of the coming of the kingdom that distinguishes Christian ethics—two thousand years after the death of Christ—from the ethics of the New Testament. That the kingdom is both future and realized is a normative part of gospel preaching, but the accentuation and interrelation of the two themes may shift to fit the way the community in history experiences itself as people of God. A changed perspective on the end time may entail a changed understanding of the roles and relationships of individuals within the community, as well as of the role of the community itself in the world. The recognition of such a difference has significance for the way we understand Paul's definition of the Christian's relationship to human institutions such as marriage.

Both celibacy and marriage derive their essential meaning for the Christian from their relationship to the community of faith. Paul's letters provide a critique of views of sexual relations, marriage commitments, and even parenthood which exalt the fulfillment of the two individual spouses and interpret the purpose and justification of marriage in terms of their interpersonal relationship alone. New Testament ethics is thoroughly communal. Does life in either state enhance or detract from one's capacity for "undivided devotion to the Lord" (1 Cor. 7:35)? To Paul, the relatively unencumbered celibate life facilitates service to the body of Christ, taken as an entity with a very brief historical future and a very pressing duty of religious conversion and preparation. To later generations of Christians, celibacy may continue to be an important witness to the radical nature of the kingdom and its demands, and to the provisional character of temporal commitments. But the union of the married couple may also constitute a fellowship that serves the community in devotion to the Lord. Paul himself suggests that the faithfulness of a believer can "consecrate" an unbelieving spouse, thus making their children "holy" (1 Cor. 7:14). The "good order" in the community which Paul hoped to promote primarily through celibacy (1 Cor. 7:35) requires a different form of service if the body must persevere and maintain its identity and mission through the generations and in enduring networks of relationship to the world. Life and growth in the contemporary church, beyond those envisioned by Paul, might be accomplished through the professional vocations of church members; the witness of marital fellowship, in addition to the tes-

timony of celibacy; the incorporation in community of the children
of Christians; and of course the institutionalization of the church
itself, with various informal or formal structures of authority, teaching, worship, and mission.

SUBMISSION OF WOMEN

A crucial question in normative ethics always is the method by
which to proceed from a general moral perspective to concrete
norms. Paul's moral perspective is furnished by his theme of incorporation in Christ by the Spirit. Stated in global terms, morally
commendable conduct is that which "builds up" the community.
But a key question is, What are to be the criteria of "upbuilding"?
Until it is supplied with more specific content, this general norm
will not be of much use in moral decision making. We move a bit
further in the direction of specificity if we agree that Paul certainly
intends to say that love and service, witness to non-Christians, and
conversion build up the community. But this does not go far enough.
Which is the "loving" act, the one that genuinely "serves" and "witnesses"? The message of Pauline epistles on this point may be that
the specific act or way of life must be judged in relation to the needs
of the concrete historical community, although insofar as that community is identified with Christ and formed in the Spirit its nature
will have a constant foundation.

We have seen that one way Paul gives content to his view of the
moral life is to borrow material from non-Christian sources (e.g.,
lists of virtues and vices, or culturally accepted social distinctions).
He then integrates this material with his body of Christ imagery.
Such material lends concreteness to his normative and exhortative
descriptions (*paraklēsis*) of Christian community. If we take the morally specific material away completely by relativizing it to the
"ethos" of Paul's time, then we are left with only a vague ideal. On
the other hand, the normativity of a biblical text or block of material
cannot be identified too closely with examples that are not its main
point. A recurring difficulty in the interpretation of Pauline texts
is that they often contain examples or substantive elaborations that
the author has assimilated from non-Christian traditions or from
social custom, with little or no critical reworking.

The two texts in 1 Corinthians on the subordination of women in the order of public worship (1 Cor. 11:2–16; 14:34–35) are good examples of the problem. As has been remarked, the theme of 1 Corinthians is the upbuilding and harmony of the Christian church, which is the necessary foundation of its realization of and witnessing to the new life in the Spirit. Paul gives a key to the interpretation of these passages when he states at the outset that he is delivering "the traditions" that are to be maintained in the faithful community (1 Cor. 11:2). The context of chapters 11–14 is a reply to various liturgical abuses in the Corinthian church. Some innovations may even have resulted from Paul's own gospel of Christian freedom (Gal. 3:28).[15] It is clear that Paul in his reply to the practices at Corinth is relying to some extent on a consensus about what is customarily thought to be "fitting" when the community comes together for worship: women are to have their heads covered in church. Such customs, of course, did not originate with Christianity, but were taken over from Judaism. The second text (1 Cor. 14:34–35, very possibly an interpolation[16]) disagrees with the first about whether women are also to keep silent in church, or whether it is taken for granted that women were involved in public prayer and prophecy (11:5). Such involvement would have represented a startling departure from Jewish tradition. Whether or not both texts were written by Paul, they both have achieved canonical status, and hence a place in the reflection of the church.

In 1 Corinthians 11, Paul states that "the head of every man is Christ, the head of a woman is her husband, and the head of Christ is God" (1 Cor. 11:3). He goes on to prescribe that a man should pray with head uncovered, while "any woman who prays or prophesies with her head unveiled dishonors her head" (v. 5). As explanation, he adds that the man is "the image and glory of God; but woman is the glory of man" (v. 7), for woman was "made from" and "created for" man (v. 8).

Several scholars understand Paul's remarks in terms of a concern to maintain the gender difference established in Genesis.[17] He adopts cultural expressions of that difference to fill in its meaning at the substantive or practical level. But while most agree that Paul affirms male and female differences, there is some dispute about whether Paul reads "difference" in terms of *hierarchy* or of *equal authority*. Most interpreters, it seems, find it regrettably necessary to concede that in matters of church order Paul did not realize fully his own vision of Christian equality and freedom. Paul K. Jewett takes the position that there simply may have been an ambivalence in the mind of Paul himself about the degree to which the historical community could realize the eschatological vision of the baptismal formula in Gal. 3:28,[18] in which are overcome human divisions and opposition (recall Genesis 3). Jewett accepts the possibility of two unharmonized themes in the passage.[19]

1 Corinthians 11 does appear to be premised upon the expectation that women will participate in public worship but this does not preclude the leadership of men. Paul intends that the relation of the sexes conform to the order that God established in the creation and upon which the new order of the church is built. Just as the customs of long and short hair, covered and uncovered heads, seem "natural" to Paul, so may a hierarchy relating male and female. Paul does seem to presuppose a subordinationist interpretation of Gen. 2:21–23 in his assertion that "The male did not come from the woman, but the woman from the male" (1 Cor. 11:8). The insight of today's theologian into the nature of the created order, and the forms in which it ought to be embodied, may differ from that of Paul. John Meier goes so far as to suggest that 1 Corinthians 11 represents simply a rationalization of already existing practices or "traditions." Like some attempts in our day to exclude women from ordination, Paul's "reasons" exemplify the cynic's definition of "theology": "church practice in desperate search for a theoretical justification."[20]

Jerome Murphy-O'Connor has provided an alternative and more generous reading of this text by focusing on the notions of authority, signs of authority, and the ordered exercise of authority. Murphy-O'Connor argues that Paul is not concerned with hierarchy, but with *equal authority* exercised through the differentiation of sexual roles established in Genesis. Customary men's and women's hair-styles are symbols of sexual differences, not necessarily of subordination. Murphy-O'Connor's central thesis is that men and women have equivalent authority to pray and prophesy in the new creation in Christ, but must fulfill these liturgical offices in ways that respect their differences. Paul associates "masculine" short hair and "feminine" long hair as signs of these differences. Although he seems to accept uncritically some first-century customs, he offers at a more profound level an eschatological critique of the deeper values of his age, since he affirms equal exercise of authority through different gender roles.[21]

Murphy-O'Connor's interpretation connects today's concern for cooperation of women and men in church and in society with what he claims the author of the biblical text explicitly intended in writing it. But if the possibility remains that Paul did understand the difference of the sexes to entail the higher authority of the male, we are left with the unresolved question of the relevance of that view to later communities. For instance, even if the Greek original behind 1 Cor. 11:10 can be translated "wears authority on her head," and this is a strong possibility,[22] the problem remains of whose authority the hairstyle or veil represents (her own or her husband's). Does a normative New Testament position in favor of the equality of men and women stand or fall with a demonstration that a particular biblical author shared a twentieth-century concern for the recognition of ecclesiastical and liturgical equality?

Beside the problems internal to 1 Corinthians 11, there stands the fact of chapter 14, in which women are told to keep quiet in church, and to put any questions to their husbands when they get home (1 Cor. 14:33–36; cf. 1 Tim. 2:8–15). This evidently is inconsistent with the order of worship presupposed in 1 Corinthians 11.[23] Chapter 14 endorses the conventions of a period in which women were not allowed to speak in legal or political assemblies, and in which household members, including wives, were ordered under the authority of the husband and father.[24] The instructions for women in 1 Corinthians 14 may have been added during an editing of the Pauline letters in light of "the growing concerns for 'good order'" in churches whose constituencies and interests were shifting.[25]

Even if 1 Corinthians 14 is an interpolation of common practice, however, the interpreter who wrestles with the normative significance of the passage still must deal with the reality of its presence in the canon. Although certain elements or modes of expression in the text may be attributable to the ethos of the original author and audience, it is difficult to argue that a passage traditionally recognized by the faith community as belonging to its "Scripture," and thus as having authority for the church, is simply to be rejected as culturally relative or wrongheaded. The task remaining after the cultural determination of the text has been recognized by a process of comparison both with other cultural, non-Christian expectations or practices (with which it is consistent) and with other central themes in the letter in which it stands—in the Pauline corpus, in the New Testament, and in the biblical canon (with which it is inconsistent)—is to decide what is its final authority, and on what grounds that may be established.

To speak of central or authoritative, as opposed to marginal or nonnormative, biblical themes is to raise again the question of standards brought *to* the Bible for use in the evaluation of materials in it. Why is it, for example, that the Christian theologian or ethicist decides that subordinationist themes are nonessential—egalitarian themes are perhaps less obvious—even though they seem central? It is impossible and undesirable to escape reference not only to contemporary experience in a general sense, but more specifically, to philosophical reflection on the dignity of the human person as male and female, or to factual evidence of the equal ability of males and females to take positions of leadership. In the case of 1 Corinthians, it may be maintained that the assignment of inconspicuous roles to women in the community assembled for worship (whether in chapter 11 or 14) is not even in keeping with the main thrust of the letter, nor with Paul's general principle of the equality of persons in Christ (Gal. 3:28), nor with his actual inclusion of women in leadership roles in his churches.[26] In 1 Corinthians Paul advises (*paraklēsis*) the members of the community to mutual love and service within harmonious relationships in keeping with the created order and with their re-creation in Christ.

I maintain, then, that what a text *means* normatively for ethics in the ongoing life of the church need not be contingent in all respects on what it originally *meant*, since it is possible and legitimate to accept a development or adaptation of meaning controlled by the text. Such a possibility is implied by Paul's own communal reference for moral evaluation. As part of his exhortation to build up the community, Paul advises, "Test everything; hold fast what is good" (1 Thess. 5:21–22).[27] It is the pilgrim community itself that is the constant in moral evaluation in light of the gospel. The Scriptures as the revealed word of that community form a point of contact, a medium of continuity, between the primitive community and our own. But they always are received from the particular perspectives of particular Christian generations, for all of whom Paul speaks when he expresses his faith that he has "the Spirit of God" (1 Cor. 7:40). Also appropriate for subsequent communities is Paul's willingness to draw conclusions, along with his modesty in claiming for them endorsement by the Spirit, evident in his care in distinguishing his own interpretations from what "the Lord" has said (e.g., 1 Cor. 7:10, 12).

DIVORCE: A MODEL OF INTERPRETATION

Paul's handling of divorce in 1 Cor. 7:10 is a case in point. This text represents the adaptation of authoritative teaching in community, and is important in several ways. First, Paul recognizes that, even in uttering a clear moral prohibition, Jesus may not define all of the particular instances to which his central insight must be applied. Paul therefore understands himself as free and responsible to add exceptions to the original negative norm. Second, the standard for applying the moral norm, and hence for making exceptions to it, is communal existence. The moral life, including the states of life which institutionalize sexual activity, is to be judged by a *communal criterion*. Paul's fundamental and characteristic stress on the community grounds the hermeneutical principle applied in his discussion of divorce; it is confirmed in parallel discussions in the Gospels of Matthew, Mark, and Luke. The Christian moral life makes sense in community; and it is in light of communal needs that authoritative moral norms may be reinterpreted.[28] Paul's saying on divorce is one of five in the New Testament (Mark 10:1–12; Matt. 5:32; 19:1–12; Luke 16:18; 1 Cor. 7:10–11). All repeat a saying of Jesus against divorce, but three make exceptions in the application of the norm (Matthew in both instances, and Paul).[29] Mark 10:6–9 and Matt. 19:4–6 have in common a reference back to the Genesis creation narratives (in a conflated quotation from Gen. 1:27 and 2:24), to which they relate Jesus' prohibition. Since at creation, God has "made them male and female," they "shall become one." "What therefore God has joined together, let no man put asunder" (Matt. 19:6; or "not man," Mark 10:9).[30] Matthew (5:32 and 19:9) differs

from Luke and Mark in that Matthew in each case adds the controverted "except for unchastity" (*porneia*) to the prohibition of di-
vorcing one's wife.

The most widely debated issue with regard to the evangelists'
treatment of divorce is the circumstances under which it is allowed
by Matthew, who directs his exception to a community combined
of Jewish and Gentile converts. The circumstance defining the
exceptional case is *porneia*, a Greek word which can signify a range
of meanings: "prostitution," "fornication," "unchastity," "indecency." Sexual infidelity or "adultery" cannot be the immorality or
indecency (*porneia*) that Matthew has in mind, since Matthew knew
and used a distinct word for adultery (*moicheia*) which does not appear here.[31] One possibility is that what is to be allowed is the
dissolution of "marriages" probably made prior to the conversion of
one or both partners, but which were originally not valid, since
there existed impediments of blood relationship. *Porneia*, then, could
be a type of incest.[32] If so, Matthew's exceptive clause would apply
to those converts whose previously contracted marriages violate the
Levitical kinship laws.

John Donahue allows that there exist serious arguments against
this equation of *porneia* with marriage between close kin.[33] But even
if incest is not the precise issue at stake, it is plausible to suggest
that Matthew's community, like Paul's, faced pastoral problems with
"mixed marriages" between Christian converts and those who did
not want to become Christian. Whatever the exception Matthew
may have had in mind,

> Matthew's position on divorce represents a dialectic of handing
> on and affirming the apodictic prohibition of divorce which he
> received from the tradition and at the same time adapting it to
> pastoral conclusions. . . . Virtually all New Testament scholars
> would admit that Matthew represents some kind of exception of
> an absolute prohibition of divorce.[34]

Paul's discussion of divorce resembles that of Matthew in important respects. First of all, Paul addresses a community that includes both Jews and Gentiles, and one in which converts might be
married to pagans. Second, Paul too reformulates Jesus' teaching.
He explicitly distinguishes the absolute saying of "the Lord" that
the married should not separate or divorce, then adds the comment

that if they do, they should become reconciled or at least not remarry (1 Cor. 7:10–11).[35] He then proceeds to make special provisions for Christians who have not initiated a separation, but with whom an "unbelieving partner" refuses to live; "in such a case the brother or sister is not bound" (7:15). ("Divorce" and "separation" are used interchangeably by Paul.) Thus, both Paul and Matthew allow adjustment of or exceptions to the original clear saying of Jesus against divorce to meet the life situations of their churches.

These accommodations of the teachings of Jesus come into better focus if we situate them in respect to the New Testament premise of the reign of God, inaugurated in Jesus in the present, and awaiting fulfillment in the future. In 1 Corinthians, Paul explicitly presses the question: What is the significance for the Christian church of its status as the community of the end time? A consistent theme in Gospel presentations of the teaching of Jesus is the proclamation of the advent of the kingdom, which the Gospel authors present in Jesus' own words and deeds. The sayings on divorce are integral to the depiction of the kingdom as present and accessible, including the restoration of the created complementarity, harmony, and unity of male and female. In Mark 10 and Matthew 19, Jesus refers to Genesis 1 and 2. Although marriage itself has a provisional character in the New Testament (Mark 12:25, "For when they rise from the dead, they neither marry nor are given in marriage, but are like angels in Heaven"), and in Paul's eyes is secondary to preparation for the kingdom, nevertheless the partnership of man and woman is presupposed and its institutionalization is reaffirmed for the temporal community. Matthew's use of a divorce saying in Jesus' Sermon on the Mount (5:27–32) puts Christian marriage in the realm of the "kingdom present." It is an ideal that is neither impossible nor utopian, nor yet an absolute moral prescription; but it is realizable *to the extent* that the gospel is heard and heeded among the faithful.[36] That the ideal is *never* accomplished perfectly is a fact the community must take into account in structuring the lives of its members.

Donahue suggests that it is precisely Paul's eschatological vision that moves him to permit divorce in some cases. The Christian is not "bound" ("a slave"), and is reminded that "in peace God has called you" (1 Cor. 7:15). "In 1 Corinthians Paul allows divorce because the presumed unharmonious marriage creates a situation where the peace or *shalom* which is characteristic of the new age, and is the fruit of Christ's saving work, cannot exist."[37] George MacRae even concludes that the preservation of the eschatological integrity of Jesus' teaching *requires* its adaptation to changing communal situations and perceptions of values, for it is only under the aegis of reinterpretation that reappropriation in each new age can proceed.[38]

Scholarly consensus solidly supports the inferences that not only an absolute prohibition of divorce is closest to the original saying of Jesus but also that some primitive Christian communities interpreted responsibility to that command as including some sort of "exception" to its literal force. The implication for normative Christian ethics is that authoritative moral norms ought to be based on the essential insights and concrete injunctions of the Bible (e.g., Genesis, Mark, and Luke); but that the authoritative and canonical collection itself constitutes a model for the developmental "handing on" (*paradosis* = *traditio*) and modification of specific moral norms (e.g., Matthew and Paul).

The themes of *community* and *eschatology* so important in New Testament references to the moral life will be key elements in the paradigm the New Testament provides for Christian ethics. The Christian community is the body of Christ that makes present in its life, as did Jesus in his, the reign of God. Ethical reflection proceeds in confidence that gift of the Spirit enables continuous and consistent discernment of the will of God within the existence of the community. This discernment is both of the renewal of the creation as expression of God's original intention and of the new covenant and its call to fidelity as the people of God. Further, it encompasses both the "fruits" which generally characterize the faithful community, and *specific* morally "right and wrong" acts and decisions that "build up" or destroy that community.

The eschatological horizon of Christianity means that the community as present kingdom always will entail radical witness in personal conduct (e.g., celibacy) and in concrete relations among persons (e.g., self-sacrificial love). (Paul, for instance, paints a striking picture of the endurance and humility required of the Christian in 1 Cor. 4:9–13). The eschatological horizon also means that the kingdom awaits fulfillment by God's definitive judgment and act. The eschaton (end time) stands in criticism of every present moral value and norm; by its standard, humans are not only finite in their perceptions and projects, but also sinful. Yet in spite of the eschatological *critique*, the Christian community enjoys the eschatological *reality* of the relation to the Father which Jesus initiates in his own life and in the existence of all whom the Spirit incorporates in the Lord. It is therefore with a remarkable confidence that Paul writes to the Thessalonians,

> May the God of peace himself sanctify you wholly; and may your spirit and soul and body he kept sound and blameless at the coming of our Lord Jesus Christ. He who calls you is faithful, and he will do it." (1 Thess. 5:23–24)

The New Testament divorce texts provide the present Christian community with two insights into the function of moral norms. These build upon the Pauline demand that morality, and rules guiding morality, be defined in relation to the life of the Spirit-filled community. The first of these insights is that underlying every concrete norm and all its adaptations is a radical demand to live out of faith in the good news that forgiveness is given and that the kingdom is at hand (Mark 1:14–15). Jesus' absolute prohibition of divorce is an example of this demand and of the expectation that it will be taken seriously.[39] Uncritical tolerance and even acceptance of divorce among Christians is a denigration of this demand. The second insight is that every norm has its significance and substance in terms of the ongoing and shifting circumstances of the pilgrim people of God. The New Testament tradition of interpretation of moral teaching which has its authority from Jesus provides a model of creative faithfulness to the eschatological reality of God's reign, as radically instituted and radically incomplete. Uncritical exclusion of divorce among Christians is unfaithful to this reality, and to the humility that ought to characterize a people still in pilgrimage toward its completion.

NOTES

1. Eugene A. LaVerdiere, "The Witness of the New Testament," in *Dimensions of Human Sexuality*, ed. Dennis Doherty (New York: Doubleday & Co., 1979), 25. LaVerdiere is a New Testament scholar who provides for the

ethicist a very useful and illuminating discussion of the function of references to sexual morality in the New Testament communities. Victor Paul Furnish agrees that what matters most to Paul is *"faith enacted in love. . . in the present life of the believer and of the believing community*, and that moral exhortations specify the meaning of love in concrete cases" (*The Moral Teaching of Paul: Selected Issues* [Nashville: Abingdon Press, 1979], 22). See also Pheme Perkins, "Paul and Ethics," *Interpretation* 38/3 (1984): 268–280. She concludes, "Perhaps most fundamentally of all, Christians need constantly to be reminded of the power of the Spirit, which, as Paul knew, is already operative within the Christian community."

2. For a philosophical commentary on the importance of community for ethics, see Alasdair MacIntyre, *After Virtue* (Notre Dame, Ind.: Univ. of Notre Dame Press, 1981); for a theological one, see Stanley Hauerwas, *A Community of Character* (Notre Dame, Ind.: Univ. of Notre Dame Press, 1981).

3. J. L. Houlden, *Ethics and the New Testament* (Baltimore: Penguin Books, 1973; New York: Oxford Univ. Press, 1977), 13.

4. On the relationship of Paul's eschatology to his ethics, see Victor Paul Furnish, *Theology and Ethics in Paul* (Nashville: Abingdon Press, 1968), 115–35.

5. Leander E. Keck distinguishes the "ethos" of early Christian communities ("what is customary, habitual") from the "ethic" of a figure like Jesus or Paul, who might affirm some elements in the ethos and reject others. Keck argues that an understanding of the ethos of the New Testament is essential to an understanding of the diversity in New Testament ethics ("Ethos and Ethics in the New Testament," in *Essays in Morality and Ethics*, ed. James Gaffney [New York: Paulist Press, 1980], 29–49).

6. It is worth noting that virginity never became a criterion of full membership in the Christian churches, and was not even a prerequisite for ministry in the Pauline communities (cf. 1 Tim. 3:2; Titus 1:6). Victor Furnish even suggests that the saying "It is well for a man not to touch a woman" (1 Cor. 7:1) is a slogan *of the Corinthians*, to which Paul responds (*The Moral Teaching of Paul: Selected Issues* [Nashville: Abingdon Press, 1979], 33). Here, and in regard to the nature of the Pauline churches generally, my analysis has been furthered by the comments of Pheme Perkins.

7. Pheme Perkins has pointed out to me that Paul most likely has come under the influence of the preaching of Cynic philosophers who maintained that human relationships, such as bonds to spouse or children, tie one to the transitory realms of nature and human endeavor. For a general discussion of Paul, the Cynics, and the Epicureans, see A. Malherbe, *Social Aspects of Early Christianity*, 2d ed., enlarged (Philadelphia: Fortress Press, 1983), 22–28.

8. LaVerdiere explains that *porneia* is "a generic term whose specific meaning must be determined from the context" ("The Witness of the New Testament," in *Dimensions of Human Sexuality*, ed. Dennis Doherty [Garden City, N.Y.: Doubleday & Co., 1979], 25). Marcel Dumais discusses some Pauline uses of

the term, in the context of a treatment of premarital sex according to the New Testament ("Couple et sexualité selon le Nouveau Testament," *Eglise et théologie* 8/1 [1977]: 47–72.

9. Pheme Perkins, *Love Commands in the New Testament* (New York: Paulist Press, 1982), 1.

10. Ibid., 6.

11. Thomas Ogletree argues the importance for ethics of the fact that eschatological expectation characterizes much of the biblical literature, including some of the prophets and Matthew, Mark, and Luke. (*The Use of the Bible in Christian Ethics* [Philadelphia: Fortress Press, 1983]).

12. 1 Timothy, written in Paul's name by a second-generation disciple, emphasizes that marriage is a part of God's good creation, to be "received with thanksgiving," and "consecrated by the word of God and prayer" (1 Tim. 4:3–5).

13. Houlden, *Ethics and the New Testament*, 9–13, 66–69.

14. Ibid., 20–21.

15. John P. Meier, "On the Veiling of Hermeneutics (1 Cor. 11:2–16)," *Catholic Biblical Quarterly* 40/2 (1978): 215, 217.

16. Cf. Hans Conzelmann, *1 Corinthians*, Hermeneia (Philadelphia: Fortress Press, 1975), 237–39; Pheme Perkins, *Ministering in the Pauline Churches* (New York: Paulist Press, 1982), 56; Erhard Gerstenberger and Wolfgang Schrage, *Woman and Man* (Nashville: Abingdon Press, 1981), 167–68; and Furnish, *Moral Teaching of Paul*, 92. It also has been argued that 1 Corinthians 11 is an interpolation. See William O. Walker, Jr., "1 Corinthians 11:2–16 and Paul's Views Regarding Women," *Journal of Biblical Literature* 94/1 (1975): 94–110. Jerome Murphy-O'Connor disputes this hypothesis in "The Non-Pauline Character of 1 Corinthians 11:2–16?" *Journal of Biblical Literature* 95/4 (1976): 615–21.

17. Jerome Murphy-O'Connor, "Sex and Logic in 1 Corinthians 11:2–16," *Catholic Biblical Quarterly* 42/4 (1980): 482–500; Paul K. Jewett, *Man as Male and Female* (Grand Rapids: Wm. B. Eerdmans, 1975), 50–61; Perkins, *Ministering*, 59; Furnish, *Moral Teaching of Paul*, 97; and Meier, "On the Veiling of Hermeneutics," 217–23.

18. Gal. 3:28, of course, also claims that in it "there is neither Jew nor Greek" nor "slave nor free." Since sexual, racial, and social status are not all categories of the same type (sexual and racial status are innate, for instance), it is difficult to make normative statements about one pair of terms that apply exactly the same way to the other two. This has led to exegetical and theological difficulties. See Elisabeth Schüssler Fiorenza, *In Memory of Her: A Feminist Theological Reconstruction of Christian Origins* (New York: Crossroad, 1983), 207, 208–18 for a recent, in-depth discussion, in which it is claimed that what is obliterated in Christ is not sexual difference, but patriarchal marriage, and the importance of sexual relationships for status in the religious community.

19. Paul K. Jewett, *Man as Male and Female* (Grand Rapids: Wm. B. Eerdmans, 1975), 112–13. Jewett also observes that in his arguments for female

subordination, Paul always appeals to the second narrative, in which creation of male and female is successive (cf. 1 Cor. 11:7; 11:18; 11:10; 1 Tim. 2:12–13). Jewett raises the further question of the validity of the subordinationist interpretation of Genesis 2, though it is the traditional rabbinic one (pp. 119–20). See also Krister Stendahl's comment that, in regard to the roles of the sexes, "Paul was a better theologian than implementer" ("Ancient Scripture in the Modern World," in *Scripture in the Jewish and Christian Traditions: Authority, Interpretation, Relevance*, ed. Frederick E. Greenspahn [Nashville: Abingdon Press, 1982], 208).

20. Meier, "On the Veiling of Hermeneutics," 224. Meier has concluded that Paul's ostensible but unconvincing "reasons" for requiring the veil are to maintain the created order and to protect women from the angelic powers present at worship, perhaps even from their lust (pp. 220–22).

21. Murphy-O'Connor, "Sex and Logic," 492–95. In keeping with this reading, Murphy-O'Connor takes "head" (*kephalē*) in 1 Cor. 11:3 ("the head of a woman is her husband") to mean "source," so that the man becomes the source of the woman, God the source of Christ, and Christ the source of "every man" (*pantos andros*, not *anthropos*), i.e., "every Christian." The meaning of the language which has resulted in the traditional (subordinationist) interpretation of 11:3 seems not to be disputed widely by other scholars; Murphy-O'Connor tries to make the case that unusual renderings of *kephalē* and *andros* are plausible translations. His argument here seems more tenuous, if only because it flies more directly in the face of the present consensus. I shall have to leave any definitive resolution to those better versed in Hebrew and Greek.

22. Cf. Jewett, *Man as Male and Female*, 56.

23. Perkins, *Ministering*, 55. Cf. Furnish, *Moral Teaching of Paul*, 101–2.

24. Perkins, *Ministering*, 55. Cf. Furnish, *Moral Teaching of Paul*, 87–89. See also Malherbe, *Social Aspects of Early Christianity*, 60–91; and Raymond E. Brown, "New Testament Background for the Concept of Local Church," in *The Catholic Theological Society of America Proceedings* 36 (1981): 7–8, for discussions of the ways in which Pauline ethics are influenced by the "house church" structures of early Christianity. A general study of the social setting of the Pauline communities is Wayne A. Meeks, *The First Urban Christians: The Social World of the Apostle Paul* (New Haven, Conn.: Yale Univ. Press, 1983).

25. Perkins, *Ministering*, 56. The same sort of concerns led to increasing use of "household code" passages in later letters such as Colossians, Ephesians, the Pastorals, and 1 Peter.

26. Furnish, *Moral Teaching of Paul*, 102–12; Schüssler Fiorenza, *In Memory of Her*, 160–204.

27. Paul W. Gooch argues that Paul himself encourages freedom in the interpretation of religious authority ("Authority and Justification in Theological Ethics: A Study in 1 Corinthians 7," *Journal of Religious Ethics* 11/1 [1983]: 62–74).

28. Cf. Furnish, *Moral Teaching of Paul*, 17.

29. In a balanced and helpful synthesis of recent exegetical studies of the divorce texts ("Divorce: New Testament Perspectives," *The Month* 14/4 [1981]: 113–20), John R. Donahue points out that

> from the perspective of tradition history there are three relatively in-
> dependent sources for Jesus' teaching on divorce; the Q tradition rep-
> resented by Luke 16:18 and Mt. 5:32; the Markan tradition of 10:1–12
> (followed by Mt. 19:1–12); and the Pauline citation of a command of
> the Lord in 1 Cor. 7:10–11. No one of these sayings agrees exactly with
> any other and all appear in different contexts. (p. 113)

One of the differences among the texts is the ways in which they link remarriage to the prohibition of divorce. It generally is agreed that what is at issue in all is the prerogative of dissolving an existing marriage, which would entail the possibility of remarriage. The texts simply are not directed at the question of the civil divorce or separation of individuals who still consider themselves to be married under religious law. Another difference is the context in which the inquiry about divorce is posed to Jesus. Luke isolates the prohibition from any introduction specifying why divorce is an issue, but Mark and Matthew put the question on the lips of Pharisees. This raises the problem of whether the discussion presupposes a Jewish practice of divorce. The question may refer to a debate then current between the schools of Rabbi Hillel and Rabbi Sham-mai. The former taught that a man could divorce his wife for any reason what-soever, while the latter interpreted Deut. 24:1 to mean that the wife had to be guilty of sexual indecency. Cf. Donahue, "Divorce: New Testament Perspec-tives," 115; Myrna Kysar and Robert Kysar, *The Asundered: Biblical Teachings on Divorce and Remarriage* (Atlanta: John Knox Press, 1978), 40; David Atkinson, *To Have and Hold: The Marriage Covenant and the Discipline of Divorce* (Grand Rapids: Wm. B. Eerdmans, 1979), 106. Joseph Fitzmyer claims to have found evidence in the recently recovered Qumran Scrolls that at least among some Jews of Jesus' time, divorce was not permitted at all (Joseph A. Fitzmyer, *To Advance the Gospel: New Testament Studies* (New York: Crossroad, 1981), 79–111). Fitzmyer takes Jesus' prohibition of divorce and remarriage in any cir-cumstances, for male and female, to be a teaching not necessarily radically discontinuous with the interpretations by his contemporaries of the Torah.

30. Matthew 5 does not refer to Genesis. It may be speculated from this that of the earliest two sources, Mark and Q, Mark alone contained a citation of Genesis. Luke selected only the Q version of the saying of Jesus, and thus does not quote Genesis; while Matthew included both versions.

31. Fitzmyer, *To Advance the Gospel*, 92–99. For another discussion, see Bruce Vawter, "The Divorce Clauses in Mt. 5, 32 and 19, 9," *Catholic Biblical Quarterly* 16 (1954): 155–67; idem, "The Biblical Theology of Divorce," *Proceedings of the Catholic Theological Society of America* (1967): 223–43; idem, "Divorce and the New Testament," *Catholic Biblical Quarterly* 39 (1977): 528–42.

32. Fitzmyer, *To Advance the Gospel*, 89, 97.

33. Donahue, "Divorce: New Testament Perspectives," 116. The Christian church did not in fact follow the definition of excluded marriages that was based on the kinship laws of Leviticus, and even the rabbinic interpretations of *zenut* attributes to it several additional meanings.

34. Ibid., 116.

35. Ibid., 117. This is likely Paul's own comment, since no other parallels associate it with Jesus.

36. Cf. Joachim Jeremias, *The Sermon on the Mount*, Facet Books 2 (Philadelphia: Fortress Press, 1963).

37. Donahue, "Divorce: New Testament Perspectives," 117. See Brian Byron, "1 Cor. 7:10–15: A Basis for Future Catholic Discipline on Marriage and Divorce," *Theological Studies* 34/3 (1973): 429–45.

38. George W. MacRae, S. J., "New Testament Perspectives on Marriage and Divorce," in *Divorce and Remarriage in the Catholic Church*, ed. Lawrence G. Wrenn (Paramus, N.J.: Newman Press, 1973), 12–13. Cf. Keck, "Ethos and Ethics in the New Testament," 44–5.

39. See Jeremias, *Sermon on the Mount*.

— 5 —

GENDER ROLES:
The Bible and
Beyond

There are many resources that both Testaments can provide for a normative picture of male-female relationships. We have examined a few of those that are key, and to which reference has been made most frequently throughout Christian tradition. Even though our study has by no means been exhaustive, it is readily apparent that these resources may be difficult to harmonize. Many questions that propelled our reading of them still remain. Are the roles of the sexes in the perpetuation of the race, the care of creation, and the upbuilding of Christian community to be equal but differentiated, complementary but hierarchical, or identical and interchangeable? Can the biblical materials, despite their diversity, guide us toward a conclusion? Will it be necessary to draw on sources beyond the Bible? If so, what are they?

To recapitulate, an initial biblical witness is given in the multi-faceted creation accounts. Recent research on Genesis 1 suggests that its author saw the function of woman and of sexuality as primarily procreative. The textual association of both male and female with the "image of God," however, precludes any normative understanding that denies to either sex full human status. Genesis 2 does not explicitly associate sex with procreation, and portrays the man and woman as companions and helpers without specifying the form that their cooperation should take. The etiological interests evidently behind Genesis 3 are answered with a characterization of actual, historical role divisions and hierarchy as connected with sin.

We find little in these chapters of Genesis about the ideal differentiation of roles, though the fact that humanity is essentially constituted as two different sexes destined for physical and social cooperation implies that some gender differentiation ought to be part of the continuing hermeneutic of the text. God's constitution of humanity in two sexes implies not only that this distinction is necessary for humanity's completion but also that it is part of the human creature's good, appropriate, and blessed finitude. The theme of "embodiedness," which has received considerable attention in recent theology and ethics,[1] militates against any "new dualism" in which physical forms and differences have no correspondence with cognitive or affective characteristics. Arguments that the sexes must in principle be identical in all characteristics and capacities seem to presuppose that sexual differentiation is merely accidental in relation to some human essence abstracted from the physical forms in which it invariably must be realized. Refusal to come to terms with the boundaries and possibilities that frame and make possible human choices is precisely the sin that propels the disaster of Genesis 3.

Identification of the sexes in distinction from one another, however, need imply neither rigid and mutually exclusive role definitions nor sexual hierarchy. Yet, in 1 Corinthians, Colossians, Ephesians, 1 Peter, and the pastorals (1 Timothy and Titus), different and definite social role assignments and hierarchy are precisely what is found. The sexual subordination promoted in both Old and New Testaments appears to reflect the social institutions of ancient Israel, and the Roman and Hellenistic cultures in which Christianity was first institutionalized. At variance with it are the ministry of Jesus and the practice of at least some of the early Christian churches.[2] Still, it remains a fact that included among "biblical" or "canonical" views of the relative roles of women and men are ones that are hierarchical. It would be difficult to argue, furthermore, that Christian tradition has not, by and large, supported patriarchy, though there have been exceptional instances of female leadership. In recent decades the Christian tradition of patriarchy has come under fire, as it has in certain periods in the past.[3]

The questions of sex differences, gender identity, gender roles, and gender relationships must be investigated honestly, and, to the extent possible, in freedom from concealed political or social agendas, whether conservative or revisionist. To avoid the issue of the psychological and social implications of sexual differentiation because of anticipation that its answer will lead to the social subordination of one sex is already to accept the premises of "sexism" that the characteristics of one sex are inferior to those of the other, that any psychological or cognitive differences whatsoever will entail discrete social role assignments, and that full humanity cannot be realized in and through the gender identity of both sexes.

THE DESCRIPTIVE AND
THE NORMATIVE

Twentieth-century attempts to come to terms with sexual differences and to redefine gender roles are marked by the immense importance which typically is given to the empirical sciences, including physiology, psychology, sociology, and anthropology. These sciences clarify the substance about which normative reflection concerns itself, although they do not as such yield moral norms. This is not to say, of course, that the methods of such sciences are undirected by evaluative presuppositions. Even the most "objective" attempts to collect and organize observations of fact can proceed only on the basis of some sort of interpretative principles. The scientist as well as the ethicist ought to be sensitive to the biases, or at least commitments, that furnish empirical investigations with their shape and direction.

One reason that the empirical sciences are important for Christian ethics is that they undergird critical perspectives on the other sources of ethics. They provide standards by which to test the adequacy of the latter to human reality in history. The Christian tradition, for instance, has been heavily inclined toward subordinationist interpretations of the Genesis creation accounts, owing both to faulty interpretation and to uncritical acceptance of cultural norms. We are encouraged to be critical of this tradition. For one thing, the tools of historical research and literary criticism have enlarged our access to the biblical authors' anthropologies and to the integral significance of the texts. In addition, empirical evidence can be supplied to highlight the experiential basis of certain values or norms, such as equality of man and woman. Both have been underplayed in the tradition *and* in the faith communities in which its symbols and foundational myths originated. Empirical studies may thus challenge received interpretations of "the normatively human," even when biblically grounded, and facilitate their modification and development. The dialogue between text, tradition, and contemporary interpreter is fruitful precisely because of such mutually correcting variations of value and insight. The contemporary struggle to understand and redefine gender roles is a good example of the productive interplay in changing cultural contexts between "biblical," "descriptive," and "normative" accounts of "the human."

The methods of the human sciences can be applied both to the Old and New Testament communities, as well as to later phases in the tradition, including our own. In the first instance, an analyst, using methods of social-scientific investigation for example,[4] might make reference to the sorts of social milieus in which male and female roles were defined in the periods in which a text originated, was developed, and was edited into written form. The modern physical and psychological sciences have provided tools with which to explore the possibility of innate bases for actual differences in male and female behavior and roles. They improve our understanding of the degree to which these differences are the products of socialization. In part this research consists of the study of individuals so as to discover in them common male or common female qualities or the absence of same (physiological, psychological). The enterprise involves cross-cultural anthropological and sociological studies of the ways in which the social roles of man and woman, and the social arrangements or institutions that support them, are generally the same; and of those in which they may vary from one culture or social situation to another. The results thus far are inconclusive but intriguing. They complement the ethicist's attempt to discern in Genesis some pattern of relationship that represents the "design of creation," in the light of which the Christian community can construe normative female and male cooperation, and evaluate present and past expectations for the sexes, including even those of other biblical authors and communities. In appealing to descriptive studies as one warrant among others in normative ethics, the ethicist hopes, indeed assumes, that observation of actual human persons and societies can support inductions about human "nature." The faith community's normative perspective also has as its referent this same nature, understood as created by God to serve God's purposes, as subject to distortion or corruption, and as called to and having potential for restoration.

MODELS OF APPROPRIATION OF
EMPIRICAL EVIDENCE

Some contemporary philosophers have adopted a phenomenological approach to the correlation of normative constructions with the actual human experience of male and female differences. Others refer to more directly empirical and quantitative studies. Both of these methods are in contrast to those that function at a relatively high level of abstraction from concrete experience. In the latter, normative understandings of gender identity and sexuality evolve within theological and philosophical anthropologies that aim for formal consistency among ideal definitions of human intelligence and freedom, physical functions and capacities, and social roles and institutions.

The Aristotelian-Thomistic natural law tradition of ethics exemplifies the abstract, formal approach in some respects. Aristotle himself, however, and to a lesser degree Thomas, defined human characteristics through an essentially empirical process of observation, reflection, and abstraction. The heightened self-critical sense of historically conscious modern philosophers leads them to contemplate the possibility that their "observations," like those of their predecessors, are shaped from a particular social and cultural vantage point. Indeed many conclude that the adoption of some particular world view is inevitable and, moreover, indispensable to the meaningful interpretation of experience, that is, to knowledge. The disturbing question is not whether all knowledge of the human is necessarily perspectival. It is whether it is credible to presume or argue any longer that there is a real and objective referent for anything like the traditional concept of "essential human nature."[5]

An inductive analysis of concrete elements in human experience presents a disadvantage which can be turned to advantage once the intrinsic fallaciousness of a one-sidedly abstract approach to "nature" is recognized. Concrete individuals and societies never represent in pure form the "essentially" or "genuinely" human. Reason abstracting from the particular will have always to take account of the limits of any one actuality from which it begins, and so to recognize that the ideal types that it constructs are to an extent human fabrications within a given socio-cultural perspective. The advantage of induction from the specific to the hypothetically universal is that it provides an opportunity to take into account the concrete interaction of nature and culture often posited in theories about humanity. Not only the individual persons and societies to be considered but also the theorizer himself or herself moves within the determinate boundaries of a time and a place and a history.

An inductive phenomenology of the sexes is exemplified by Abel Jeanniere's study of the differentiation of masculine and feminine as a reciprocal relation realized historically, socially, and culturally. Even though there exist certain constant biological factors, such as the male's phallic sexuality and the female's capacity for pregnancy, still femininity and masculinity will never be defined finally and "objectively," since even the constants are susceptible of different forms of cultural recognition and hence different modes of integration in personal and social life.[6]

It is possible also for the philosopher or theologian to appeal to descriptive accounts of a more precise and quantifiable sort. Mary Midgley takes up the issue whether there is a set of universal characteristics that can be said to separate "man" from the animals. She is not hesitant to face up to ethological studies that contest that the philosophical preference for viewing human "nature" as a unique reality, with more or less knowable and definable limits, is not borne out clearly by empirical evidence.

Midgley emerges from this confrontation convinced that the natures of "man" and animal converge, but that this is no affront to the dignity of her own species. Human nature does not involve features, such as rationality and language, that are unparalleled in animals. Rather, what is "really characteristic" of humans is "the shape of the whole cluster" of properties that they possess.[7] The most striking feature of Midgley's account is her fundamental and unusual willingness to construe positively and without defensiveness the implications of research indicating that voluntary behavior and patterns of social organization are grounded in, not reduced to, the animal nature of the species. It is her simple receptivity to "the evidence" that opens an avenue around the impasse at which some neo-scholastic approaches to natural law theory had arrived. The connection between empirical research and our understanding of the normatively human is reestablished because the project of defining "human nature" no longer depends on establishing *clear and distinct*, as well as *culturally transcendent*, ideas of "uniquely" human characteristics shared by all the species' normal members. Empirically based generalizations aim to provide more adequate notions of the range of possible human properties and of the arrangements into which they are likely to fall. Midgley suggests that, like the race, man and woman have distinctive ranges of characteristics and are perhaps inclined to naturally different "emotions," a term evidently denoting innate spontaneous bases of faculties more readily associated with freedom, such as affectivity, cognition, and judgment. None of these bases are possessed exclusively by one sex, and "different cannot mean inferior here."[8]

EMPIRICAL RESEARCH:
SEX AND GENDER
DIFFERENCES

The fact that it is empirically based does not make the investigation of male and female differentiation, physiological or social, less susceptible to influence by the values that the designers and interpreters of the research associate with certain outcomes. Those with feminist interests, for instance, may engage in observation and reporting of "data" to support the thesis that there exist no significant differences between male and female beside the obvious physiological ones, primarily those of the reproductive system, and that the implications of the latter for psychological and social differentiation can be minimized. Those interested in legitimating the association of the female with domestic roles, and of the male with economic ones, may focus on childbearing capacity and relative physical size, extrapolating to discrete and fairly inflexible ranges of psychological traits, and concluding that physical and psychological differences entail social roles with very small areas of convergence.

Some current research has suggested that differences between the sexes extend beyond the grossly physical to the psychological and emotional. This hypothesis gains plausibility from the fact that the human mind is not a separate entity superadded to the body, but one aspect, with corporeality, of the totality of a human individual. Some scientists have a long list of sex-related differences;[9] others are willing to consider the possibility that there are a small number of sex differences that are well established. These researchers tend to express reservations about concluding too rapidly from them to male and female roles, and see the latter as largely a product of socio-cultural typing. Eleanor Maccoby and Carol Jacklin of Stanford, who contend that most sex differences have no innate basis, still regard four such differences as statistically significant: verbal ability in girls, and visual spatial ability, mathematical excellence, and aggression in boys.[10] Nurturing behavior *may* be a further differentiating characteristic of females, but its incidence has not been well documented.[11] The research designs behind such conclusions are, of course, not beyond criticism, since no researcher ever has available a "pure" specimen of human "nature" uninfluenced by cultural expectations. Additionally, researchers themselves must always operate with some hypothesis about what they are likely to find, which directs their observations. Joseph Pleck, a sociologist and author of *The Myth of Masculinity*, argues that most research to date has been conducted according to a "Male Sex Role Identity" paradigm (MSRI) which has prevented researchers from interpreting evidence appropriately. Pleck argues that aggressiveness, for instance, is *not* an innate and typically male characteristic, nor is weak interest in caring for children. These are products of social expectations.[12]

In reviewing critically the discrepancies among the conclusions of specialists in other fields, the ethicist will recognize both the necessity of reliance on such investigations, and the inevitability of uncertainty in regard to "findings," since even empirical research involves a continual process of testing and refining hypotheses. Perhaps the best advice for the ethicist is to recognize her or his own presuppositions and implicit hypotheses, and so consider most seriously the impact that evidence unfavorable to them would have on his or her agenda. Since I presuppose the essential equality of male and female, and that they are equally competent to fulfill most if not all social roles, I will now consider the possibility that there may be some physiologically based gender differences. This possibility has empirical support that, while not universal, is wide enough to be significant.

If there is an obvious connection between male and female physiology and reproductive roles, it is not unlikely that there exists some link between reproductive systems and some less evident physical differences. These might in turn have an impact on psychology and thus on social relationships. The human brain and gender-specific hormones in both normal and abnormal individuals have been objects of research. The most obvious differences in male and female sexual development and function evidently are controlled by the brain. The brain is influenced by hormones, so that it inclines the individual toward certain behavioral characteristics, such as aggressiveness, which appears to differentiate men from women.[13] Hormones influence brain and sex-related behavior normally when they are released in increased levels at puberty. But hormones can also effect abnormal changes in fetal development or in the adult who receives hormones as part of a medical therapy. Scientific consensus also supports the conclusion that women generally have better capacities for cognitive activities controlled by the left, or verbal, hemisphere of the brain, while men stand out in those associated with the right, or visual, side. A recent study has provided some evidence that there are not only functional but also structural differences in the human male and female brains, comparable to those already verified in some other species.[14]

What does this suggest about the relation between sex-specific physiological differences and gender roles? It appears that different physical characteristics, deriving at least in part from their reproductive roles, may create in men and women a tendency toward certain emotional (nurturing, aggressive) or cognitive (verbal, visual) capacities, which may in turn influence the ways they fulfill various social relationships. This is not to say, however, that emotional and cognitive traits vary greatly between the sexes or are manifested in comparable degrees by every member of each sex; or that the fact that males and females may fulfill certain roles somewhat differently implies that each sex can fulfill only a certain set of social roles, much less the devaluing of one sort of role or set of roles, and the subordination of it to that of the opposite sex.

The problem here is to take account of the integrity of the person as body and mind or psyche, and as not a simple product of his or her environment, while avoiding crude biological determinism. As Melvin Konner puts it,

> There is in each of us a residue of characteristics of heart and mind that we brought with us when we entered the womb, a mere few days from conception. The denial of this, as liberal as it usually sounds, is really a denial of individuality, in the most fundamental sense, and it is every bit as dangerous as the most rigid forms of genetic determinism.[15]

To say basic physical forms of existence have no cognitive or affective implications seems dualistic. It separates humanity from its own biological concreteness and from other animal species. This fragmentation runs counter to our attempts on other fronts to demonstrate the unity of body and spirit and the interdependence of humanity and the rest of nature.

EMPIRICAL RESEARCH: SOCIAL SYSTEMS AND GENDER ROLES

Even though the sort and degree of gender difference substantiated by current research do not seem naturally conducive to vast disparities between male and female status and function, it is nonetheless the case that such disparities have existed, continue to exist, and might even appear to characterize all forms of human social organization. Human societies have with remarkable consistency identified males with public economic and political roles, and females with domestic and child-rearing ones.[16] Why do these discrepancies so consistently occur? Many researchers have examined a potential source of them which is as obvious as it is universal: reproductive roles that are rooted in reproductive biology.

Needless to say, the most apparent sex difference is that of the genitalia and reproductive systems. It has equally apparent implications for some fundamental variance in male and female function. Anthropologists theorize that social organization in primitive human society was divided along clear sexual lines. Females needed to be protected from attack or harm in the interest of the species, since they were the bearers and feeders of young. Males, with greater size, musculature, and visual-spatial skill, which may have evolved *because* of the male role as protector, were assigned the tasks of hunting and fighting. That early human groups generally allocated labor in these ways is not seriously in dispute among anthropologists; parallels can be cited today, not only from among the more "primitive" societies of the world, but, in more subtle forms, from among the more "advanced."

Critical questions about the *normative status* of such divisions remain nonetheless. To what extent should social roles continue to be derived from the biological roles of man and woman? Some social accommodation of the latter clearly is necessary; evident instances being the temporary circumscription of a woman's activity by childbirth and to some extent by pregnancy and the tie of a lactating mother to a nursing infant.[17] Furthermore, even if reproductive function does result in some differentiation of social roles, it is not immediately apparent why there exists considerable disparity in the social status associated with these roles.[18] Both male and female make necessary contributions to the propagation of the species, and, if anything, it is the female's that is more in evidence.

A decade ago, two anthropologists, Michele Zimbalist Rosaldo and Louise Lamphere, addressed what they took to be the obvious fact—that domestic roles for women and economic and political ones for men are cross-culturally universal.[19] Several of their collaborators probed for explanations of sexual asymmetry which might account for its apparent universality and durability, while yet allowing its contingency. To generalize, these scholars tend to suggest that pregnancy and lactation confine women to positions of social powerlessness. The key to the equality of men and women in power is the loosening of the bond between women and reproduction, childrearing, and domestic tasks, and more involvement of men. This will make possible the incorporation of women into the traditional "man's world" of public economic and political life.

More recent anthropological research suggests that it may be a mistake to begin the study and description of male and female roles and status by looking for "universal" or "essential" gender roles (deriving directly from sex differences) that transcend history and society. "Man" and "woman" cannot be understood independently, apart from their relationship and interaction in concrete social contexts.[20] Furthermore, as Rosaldo has pointed out (six years after the publication of *Woman, Culture, and Society*), studies that take "woman" (or "man") alone are often flawed by an individualist bias: it is assumed that the nature of woman as a class can be discovered by scrutinizing the typical needs, behavior, or experience of the individual female.[21] (Often a psychological, especially neo-Freudian, approach to individual female experience is used.) The psycho-social character of the individual is frequently linked with biology as effect to cause. Sex-based reproductive and mothering roles are then used to account for a cross-cultural *social* division between domestic and public spheres. Rosaldo makes it clear, however, that reproductive or physical characteristics, however universal, are not necessarily the most important defining characteristics of a woman (or man) in a particular society. Anthropologists agree that these characteristics may receive different social, political, and cultural interpretations, which can be appreciated only within a whole, concrete, social system.[22] It is fallacious, therefore, to assume that a division of public and domestic realms of influence is necessitated by reproductive roles, especially woman's supposedly "constraining" one, as though these roles were the unalterable givens which in turn account for universal social structures and social roles. Female and male biology may be universal, but the institutionalization of reproduction and parenting, and the importance attributed to these activities in relation to others, is variable for both male and female. Biological differences undoubtedly exist, and undoubtedly contribute to socially institutionalized gender roles and the cultural ideologies that "explain" them and that mediate the person's subjective experience of them. Nevertheless, these biological differences alone do not account for "gender," that is, for maleness and femaleness in a social context. As Rosaldo recommends, anthropologists and other empirical researchers need to develop tools for the study of sex and gender that permit much greater appreciation of the many *different* ways in which biology and gender roles can be interconnected, and of the many ways culture shapes their significance for both individuals and societies.

Since the publication of *Woman, Culture, and Society*, some doubts have been cast on the thesis that male supremacy is, in fact, the "universal" pattern of gender relationship, even though it certainly is predominant. Peggy Reeves Sanday, using studies of over 150 societies, has challenged the presupposition of universal female subordination that she formerly endorsed.[23] Her revised thesis is that male and female power roles vary among societies. In addition to primary sex differences, gender roles and power relations are determined by a given natural and social environment and the activities necessary to sustain the community in that environment (e.g., plant gathering and cultivation, and the raising of domestic animals versus hunting, migration, and warfare). The domination of women by men tends not to occur in societies in which the sexes mingle and cooperate in daily affairs, even though there is sexual division of labor. Regular cooperation and relative equality of the sexes occur most frequently when the environment is beneficent rather than hostile.

Martin King Whyte also demonstrates considerable variability in gender roles, at least in "preindustrial societies." Although there are no known societies in which women predominate generally over men, there are some societies patterned on equality of the sexes. In addition, there are some areas in which women typically dominate such as control over female products, children, the domestic sphere. In other areas, he concludes that equality is more typical than hierarchy. These areas include labor that contributes to basic subsistence, funeral ceremonies, sexual drives, and ability to divorce. Interestingly, although Whyte perceives greater equality as a positive and possible goal for modern society, he isolates two "universal" factors which he claims account for the unequal status of women in relation to men that is in fact prevalent. The first factor is the family, which unites man and woman in a way discouraging to female agitation for change. The second is the fact that "women everywhere have the primary burden of early child care," even though other aspects of role division may vary.[24] Since both factors derive from male and female contributions to and cooperation in reproduction, Whyte's theses about variability and potential equality reopen the question posed by Rosaldo, Lamphere, and others: If physical characteristics conduce to certain social roles, and if these characteristics and at least some of these roles are constant, how then can gender roles and male-female cooperation be redefined in ways that both account for male-female differences, and permit realization of the full potential of each sex and of the equality of the sexes? Although some anthropologists insist that even in "simple societies" genuine equality of the sexes is illusory,[25] it hardly can be denied that social roles and social relationships are variable for both sexes. The de facto prevalence of male domination as a social pattern and the sexual and reproductive physiology of males and females are "givens" for any analysis of gender roles, but the nature and degree of connection between them is far from clear.

If, as biblical and empirical studies both suggest, the implications of sexual differentiation extend beyond the minimum requirements of species propagation, then their significance must not be overinterpreted, just as it must not be ignored. Male and female "traits" are predispositions rather than determinants, and to the extent that they do characterize particular individuals they will be capable of expression in a wide range of life styles and professional commitments open to the contributions of both sexes. The exclusion of either sex from all but a few professions that require certain clear gender-related physical capacities should not be an issue. In particular neither empirical evidence nor the scriptural accounts of creation support either the thesis that the exclusive role for which women, and women alone, are suited is a domestic one, or that domestic and parental roles are intrinsically less valuable than public political and economic ones. Most human "roles" (as distinct from traits or capacities) can be fulfilled in a variety of styles. Surely both males and females share the flexibility and adaptability that characterize the species as a whole in comparison to other animals. An architect, for example, certainly relies on a certain amount of visual-spatial acuity, but also acquires much of his or her knowledge of architecture through verbal media. It is arguable that aesthetic sensitivity is more important than either verbal or visual skills. Similarly, the recent experience of many Western couples has demonstrated that men as well as women are successful at and find fulfillment in "parenting." The neologism itself represents a move beyond the sexism exemplified in the contrasting connotations of the expressions "fathering a child" and "mothering a child."

Attempts to minimize as far as possible the connection of biological difference to psychological and cognitive differences are a response to past and present sex discrimination and role limitation. It is clear, however, that the equation of human freedom with inde-terminacy reflects an extreme version of the liberal ideal of the au-tonomous agent, unconstrained—indeed undefined—by any signif-icant communal or physical boundaries. In liberal political and moral systems the social world and family relationships tend to become mere instruments through which the individual achieves autono-'mous self-actualization and enhances his or her freedom of move-ment and decision. The Genesis accounts of God's purposes in cre-ating humanity are radically at odds with such a perspective. They are equally at odds with a definition of woman in terms so confining that they entail her exclusion from the "image" that humanity shares not with the animals. And nowhere in the texts is it indicated that the command and blessing, "Be fruitful," is addressed less to the man than to the woman, nor that it should evoke a less than fully parental response.

CONCLUSIONS

A primary task of normative ethics is to encourage interpretations of gender characteristics free from the connotations of inferiority and superiority that support the institutions of sexual hierarchy over which Genesis 3 casts its shadow of judgment. This normative task must proceed from empirical foundations, since no "ideal" can make sense of or be a transformative agent for a reality to which it bears no integral connection. The empirical sciences offer conclusions drawn from observations of particular individuals or groups. De-scriptions of particular subjects are then pushed toward generali-zation, sometimes by explicit claims of universality, but often by an implicit suggestion that what is true for a representative group is true for all.

The Priestly and Yahwist stories of the creation of humans tell us essentially that sexual differentiation is part of God's design and that it is intended to serve the species and the preservation of the created order through a partnership of man and woman. It is as-sumed by the biblical authors that the differentiation of the roles of finite beings must take some concrete forms; further, in the course of human history set by the Fall, by humanity's universal departure from obedience to the Lord and hence from respect for and trust in one another, that form will be distorted. The biblical symbols of the Genesis accounts provide an etiology of hierarchy that transcends any quest of anthropologists for its concrete genesis in primitive society.[26] The Yahwist (Genesis 2) hints that sexual subordination has about it the same aura of absurdity and inexplicability as does the choice of the man and woman to heed the serpent instead of the Lord God. Humans, both male and female, have an incorrigible inclination to act in what they rather shortsightedly perceive to be their own self-interest, will reinforce and perpetuate self-serving actions by violence and guile, and when exposed to the light of righteousness will seek immediately to hide, to deny, and to blame.

The greater the degree of humanity's self-consciousness in regard to its own physical, psychological, and social makeup, the greater will be the human ability to recreate the communal and interpersonal structures through which elements in that constitution uncritically have been given expression or hindered. Mary Midgley has made the point effectively that human dignity consists not in suppressing or denigrating the physical or the innate constituents of "nature," but in relating them to human self-definition and freedom. Descriptive studies are indispensable in the attempt of normative ethics to understand what it would mean for male and female relationships to transcend those particular individual and social forms that perpetuate the onerous constraint and conflict of the sexes.[27] The application of scientific method to the differentiation of the sexes helps the ethicist to fill out substantively the biblical perspective on right order between them.

The relation between empirical research and biblical interpretation, finally, is of necessity circular. So it is with the other sources of Christian ethics. The perspective of Genesis helps us to distinguish elements, such as hierarchy, in the actual situation of man and woman that depart from the fullness of humanity as male and female. Sexual subordination presupposed, endorsed, or enjoined elsewhere in the Bible, including the New Testament, can be criticized by the cumulative criterion of Genesis 1—3. At the same time, the biblical accounts are tested not only against each other but also by their ability to summon up assent to the veracity of their interpretative recapitulation of the experience of human being in time. This is not to say that the biblical depiction of the design of the created order is normative only where it symbolizes what verifiably has been the case in history; quite the contrary, as with the equality of male and female. Rather, one criterion of its normativity is its power to criticize what historically has been the case while yet not defining the human ideal in a way essentially at odds with the window onto human characteristics and potential that the descriptive sciences provide. Criteria beyond the Bible, in turn, assist in the reappropriation of biblical symbols by showing their adequacy or inadequacy to "upbuild" human and Christian existence.

SUMMARY

Taken together in a relationship of mutual criticism, biblical views of male and female, especially those of Genesis, and empirical investigations of the human provide a normative view of the relationship between the sexes that has the following contours. Sexual differentiation as male and female is good, is part of humanity as created (human "nature"), and is not incompatible with the inclusion of both male and female in what is meant by "image of God." Sexual complementarity involves a partnership of life in the service of community—of the species and of the whole created order. An intrinsic purpose of gender differentiation, understood as a property of the race, is procreation. The fulfillment of humanity in individuals is also normative in the Christian understanding of sexuality and gender, as suiting the woman and man for mutual companionship. Sexuality and sexual difference are fully personal, not reductionistically or dualistically limited to the reproductive organs. The fact that humanity is characterized by freedom makes impossible any narrow confinement of the expression of the masculine and the feminine to propagative and species-survival functions. A human being has as such a dignity that transcends the species and the value of its maintenance, and has freedom in regard to the fulfillment of that dignity, that is, in whether to obey or disobey God's commands. God not only created Adam and Eve as individuals—setting them apart from the other creations—but also addresses them, commands them, and rebukes them as individuals in the process of creation, commissioning, temptation, fall, and punishment. It is not consistent with either creation account to extrapolate, as with other animals, in any deterministic way from biologically grounded capacities or predispositions to personal and social realizations of maleness and femaleness. In the formation of individual characters and of interpersonal and social relationships there must intervene a distinctively human sort of freedom and flexibility toward a "range" of characteristics natural to humanity. Freedom, not indeterminacy, makes humanity capable of "dominion," and makes it in "God's image" and thus set apart within the created orders.

We need normative ethics in order to reinterpret the hypothesis that male-female difference and complementarity extend beyond gross reproductive design. Empirically based descriptions of male and female may help fill in the substance of that difference. At the same time, Christian ethics must not permit experiential observation to override or replace the biblical paradigms of the integrity of the human individual as embodied and as free, and of the ideal equality of the sexes. Differences ought to be appreciated rather than denied, but not interpreted with a narrowness that excludes freedom and equality. This has been the case wherever inflexibly defined and separate psycho-social gender roles have been prescribed. I do not believe it is now, or ever will be, possible for Christian ethics to enumerate fixed normative lists of male and female characteristics and concomitant social roles. This is due both to the flexibility of the human person and to the necessarily partial, perspectival, and provisional character of all our knowledge, which increases in these qualities the more specific it becomes. Normative Christian ethics must rest content with providing a constant critique of all extant sex role definitions in the realization that conflict between the sexes will be present in history as long as is sin. It must also be conscious that the Eve and Adam who went into the world clothed in skins were the same woman and man created for partnership in the garden.

NOTES

1. James Nelson, *Embodiment: An Approach to Sexuality and Christian Theology* (Minneapolis: Augsburg Pub. House, 1978). See also idem, *Between Two Gardens: Reflections on Sexuality and Religious Experience* (New York: Pilgrim Press, 1983).

2. Elizabeth Schüssler Fiorenza and others have demonstrated quite decisively that women played leading roles in primitive Christianity, both during Jesus' lifetime and after his death. See *In Memory of Her: A Feminist Theological Reconstruction of Christian Origins* (New York: Crossroad, 1983), 105–204; and

also Elisabeth M. Tetlow, *Women and Ministry in the New Testament* (New York: Paulist Press, 1980); and the articles by Elisabeth Schüssler Fiorenza, Elizabeth Carroll, and Raymond E. Brown in *Theological Studies* 36/4 (1975).

3. Ann Oakley, in *Sex, Gender and Society* (London: Maurice Temple Smith, 1972) defines "sex differences" as natural characteristics, such as bodily strength, and "gender differences" as social roles. She observes that the question of sex differences and roles has been debated particularly in three historical periods in which the status of men and women has undergone change: the Elizabethan and Victorian eras, and the present.

4. *Interpretation* 36/3 (1982) contains four helpful articles (by Bruce J. Malina, Burke O. Long, John G. Gager, and Wayne A. Meeks) focused on the relevance of the social sciences to the interpretation of the Bible, particularly in light of the degree to which these sciences can enlarge our understanding of the sort of historical communities out of which the Scriptures arose.

5. Cf. James M. Gustafson, "Nature: Its Status in Theological Ethics," *Logos* 3 (1982): 5–23.

6. Abel Jeanniere, *The Anthropology of Sex* (New York: Harper & Row, 1967).

7. Mary Midgley, *Beast and Man: The Roots of Human Nature* (Ithaca, N.Y.: Cornell Univ. Press, 1978), 207, 326.

8. Ibid., 353.

9. Two neuropsychologists at Stanford University, Dianne McGuinness and Karl Pribram, contend that the list of significant differences between men and women is relatively long, and that these have a biological base. Men excel at spatial thinking, women at verbal; men are less sensitive to heat, but more to cold than females; females have better hearing, taste, and touch, while men have better daylight vision and poorer night vision; women have better fine motor coordination; men are more curious; women are more attentive to people and social relationships (David Gelman et al., "Just How the Sexes Differ," *Newsweek* [18 May 1981]: 73–4; Jeannie Wilson, "The Amazing Brain," *Town and Country* [August 1982]: 81).

10. Eleanor Maccoby and Carol Jacklin, *The Psychology of Sex Differences* (Stanford, Calif.: Stanford Univ. Press, 1974). Contrast this minimum with popular notions of "masculine" and "feminine" traits. Inge K. Broverman et al., conducted a survey of college students (around 1970) from which they discovered that men were perceived to manifest characteristics belonging to a "Competency Cluster," such as independence, objectivity, logicality, and business skill, as well as bluntness, roughness, and sloppiness. Women were associated with a "Warmth-Expressiveness Cluster," including literature, but also passivity, sneakiness, naiveté, and lack of ambition. It is perhaps not surprising that the masculine items were also considered by college-age lay subjects to be more "socially desirable." It is alarming that a sample of practicing mental health clinicians identified the characteristics of a "healthy man" with those of a "healthy adult," implying that a "healthy woman" is less than "healthy" by "adult" standards ("Sex Role Stereotyping: A Current Appraisal," in *Life: The*

Continuous Process: Readings in Human Development, ed. Freda Rebelsky (New York: Alfred A. Knopf, 1975), 289–302).

11. A lucid and provocative overview of the physiological bases of human behavior is Melvin Konner's *The Tangled Wing: Biological Constraints on the Human Spirit* (New York: Harper & Row, 1983). Konner presents the results of recent scientific studies, and provides abundant references to the primary literature in which they are presented. Chap. 6 is devoted to the connections between brain, hormones, and gender differences. Pp. 111–19 treat "nurturance" as a hypothetically innate characteristic.

12. Joseph Pleck, *The Myth of Masculinity* (Cambridge, Mass.: M.I.T. Press, 1981).

13. Conclusions about the role of hormones in gender differentiation based on observation of normal brains have been confirmed in studies on individuals who in some respect depart from the norms. For example, children of mothers who were given male hormones during pregnancy to prevent miscarriages scored significantly higher on a standard aggression test than did unexposed siblings (Melvin Konner, *Tangled Wing*, 123–24; Gelman et al., "Just How the Sexes Differ," 78).

14. Sex differences in animals often center in the hypothalamus, an important source of mating behavior, e.g., in rats and canaries (Melvin Konner, "She and He," *Science 82* [September 1982]: 59; Gelman et al., "Just How the Sexes Differ," 78; Wilson, "The Amazing Brain," 81). In humans, evidence has been found that tissues in the corpus collosum, the link between the brain's right and left hemispheres, differ in the sexes ("His and Hers Brains," *Science 82*, 14–15).

15. Konner, *Tangled Wing*, 105.

16. Melford E. Spiro has studied the kibbutz movement in support of the thesis that innate male and female differences predispose the sexes to more or less traditional tasks, such as child care and cooking for women. The evidence to which Spiro appeals is the fact that early kibbutzim strove to equalize male and female roles, and to encourage participation of both sexes in all areas of communal life. Kibbutz women now, however, choose to participate primarily in roles that are traditionally female. Thus sex differences, Spiro concludes, must be precultural. He criticizes the "identity" definition of sexual equality in favor of an "equivalence" one which allows for biologically based male and female differences. It is not clear, however, why basic biological differences need to result in traditional roles. Spiro's own presuppositions about the "feminine" may be revealed in his statement that in the early kibbutz movement, "It was as if the women felt that to achieve equality, with men, they had to reject their femininity" (p. 9). As examples of "feminine charm" he gives "cosmetics, beauty care, perfume, jewelry, and feminine hair styles" (p. 8). Although the kibbutz development is of interest, it must be objected that Spiro hardly has achieved a "culture-free" study group; even a good faith intention to form egalitarian communities could not overcome all sexist biases in one

generation. To this must be added the indirect influence of Jewish and Israeli cultural expectations of men and women (*Gender and Culture: Kibbutz Women Revisited* [Durham, N.C.: Duke Univ. Press, 1979]).

17. Elizabeth H. Wolgast (*Equality and the Rights of Women* [Ithaca, N.Y.: Cornell Univ. Press, 1980]) suggests that since women are not in every way like men, they do not have rights definable in precisely the same ways. Wolgast compares humans with other animal species, and locates the uniqueness of women primarily in their childbearing role; this role entails particular "rights."

18. Even in cultures in which femininity is idealized, it is difficult to argue that the real status and power of women are enhanced. Rosemary Ruether has shown that the "cult of true womanhood" merely appears to accord high social status to woman, since it functions to exclude woman from spheres of public political and economic influence by confining her to her "proper sphere"—the home ("Home and Work: Women's Roles and the Transformation of Values," *Theological Studies* 36/4 [1975]: 647–59).

19. Michele Zimbalist Rosaldo and Louise Lamphere, eds., *Woman, Culture, and Society* (Stanford, Calif.: Stanford Univ. Press, 1974).

20. Jane Monnig Atkinson, "Anthropology," *Signs* 8/2 (Winter 1982): esp. 247–58; Michelle Z. Rosaldo, "The Use and Abuse of Anthropology," *Signs* 5/3 (Spring 1980): 389–417.

21. Rosaldo, "Use and Abuse of Anthropology," 393.

22. Sherry B. Ortner and Harriet Whitehead, "Introduction: Accounting for Sexual Meanings," in *Sexual Meanings: The Cultural Construction of Gender and Sexuality*, ed. Sherry B. Ortner and Harriet Whitehead (New York: Cambridge Univ. Press, 1981), 1–27; Rosaldo gives the example of hunter-gatherer groups, in which women are identified more in terms of their sexuality and sexual activity than of motherhood ("Use and Abuse of Anthropology," 412–25; see also Jane F. Collier and Michele Z. Rosaldo, "Politics and Gender in Simple Societies," in *Sexual Meanings*, ed. Ortner and Whitehead, 275–329); Judith Shapiro, "Anthropology and the Study of Gender," *Soundings* 64/4 (Winter 1981): 446–65); and Carol P. MacCormack and Marilyn Strathern, eds., *Nature, Culture, and Gender* (New York: Cambridge Univ. Press, 1980). For a collection in which more emphasis is laid on the biological bases of social organization, see Lionel Tiger and Heather Fowler, eds., *Female Hierarchies* (Chicago: Beresford Book Service, 1978).

23. Peggy Reeves Sanday, *Female Power and Male Dominance: On the Origins of Sexual Inequality* (New York: Cambridge Univ. Press, 1981). Cf. her contribution to *Woman, Culture, and Society*.

24. Martin King Whyte, *The Status of Women in Preindustrial Societies*, (Princeton, N.J.: Princeton Univ. Press, 1978), 179.

25. For example, Collier and Rosaldo, "Politics and Gender in Simple Societies," ed. Ortner.

26. An interesting slant on Genesis 2—3 is suggested by the presence of myths of a primitive matriarchy in many societies. A common element in these

myths is an original situation in which women held the power over men, but somehow lost power, e.g., because they abused it. The myth is told to explain why men now have power over women, that is, to justify the status quo. (Joan Bamberger, "The Myth of Matriarchy: Why Men Rule in Primitive Society," in *Women, Culture, and Society*, ed. Rosaldo and Lamphere, 263–80.) The observant reader will recall that in Gen. 2:24, it is the woman who enters into debate with the serpent, abuses her freedom, and leads the man in so doing. Part of the punishment assigned her by God is that the man will "rule over" her (3:16). I think on the whole, however, Genesis 2—3 communicates a sense of an original equality, not of matriarchy or patriarchy.

27. Peggy Reeves Sanday has compared anthropological literature to study the cross-cultural incidence of rape, finding that it is a form of conflict and subjugation not "demanded by" the innate aggressiveness of males. Rape is most likely to occur in cultures in which violent behavior is encouraged in men, e.g., when a society is under constant threat by outside aggressors. Rape-free societies are ones in which women's physical functions and social contributions are valued, and in which men and women both participate in authority structures. The implication is that expressions of aggression need not be antisocial and violent, even if aggression is innately human and especially male (*Female Power and Male Dominance*, esp. pp. 183–211).

— 6 —

THOMAS AQUINAS:
Marriage, Procreation, and the Law of Nature

Ethicists are sometimes fond of citing inflammatory statements from classic sources. I will open this chapter with a few, for their abundance in St. Thomas provides an irresistible occasion for sin, even for a sympathizer. Thomas took the position that males become fully human at forty days gestation, and females not until ninety.[1] Moreover, he supplied the supposed biological disparity with metaphysical justification by saying that all babies would be male, taking after the perfect prototype of their fathers, were it not for the ill influence of "a south wind, which is moist."[2] Given this inauspicious beginning, it is not surprising that women, according to Thomas, are less rational, less suited to intellectual pursuits, and less capable of firm judgment than are men. Therefore they are naturally subject to "others wiser than themselves," to be specific, men.[3] Still, Thomas did grant that the existence of the female sex was not some quirk in the creation with which the Almighty had been incompetent to deal. The differentiation of male and female bodies, and the sexual act which unites them, are necessary to the work of reproducing the race.[4] Unfortunately, the act of conception itself has ill effects on one's capacity for a more dignified human occupation, contemplation of the truth.[5] All things considered, virginity is preferable to marriage since the former is more conducive to "thinking on the things of God" and thus to "the good of the soul."[6]

Marriage, he allows, is a state generally accompanied by sexual acts, and has procreation as its justifying reason. It is a sin to seek sexual intercourse in marriage without that intention, though a far worse one to seek it without being married at all.[7] Marriage is "excused" if the couple "compensates" for their passion and worldliness by attempting to beget children, by remaining faithful to one another, and by establishing a household and a "community of works."[8] In fact, they can even be a sign of Christ's presence to the church if they are committed as Christians to the permanent inseparability also required by the natural duty of raising up offspring.[9] One aspect of Thomas's view of marriage which frequently seems to be overlooked is his honest esteem for the intensity of love between husband and wife, which he associates with their union in "one flesh."[10] He also values their partnership in domestic life, on account of which he says that wife and husband enjoy friendship of the greatest sort.[11]

SEX AND THE
LAW OF NATURE

At the beginning of the discussion in the *Summa Theologica* on the relation between matrimony and the offices of nature, there is a concise statement of Thomas's view of the law of nature, of its authority for the moral agent, and on nature's norms for marriage. Typically enough, this summary begins, proceeds, and ends by citing Aristotle's *Ethics*. It offers that humans are by nature social animals, in both the political and connubial senses; that the natural end of society is mutual assistance; that the purpose of matrimony is the cooperation of man and woman in begetting and educating children and in managing a household; and that to male and female should be allotted those among the "works that are necessary for human life" the ones that are "becoming" to their sex.[12] Such are the dictates of human nature, discovered by reason, and formulated as a standard of virtue for all matters pertaining to sexual activity.[13] This standard is elaborated in many details in the *Summa Theologica* and *Summa Contra Gentiles*. It is added, for example, that marriage is naturally monogamous and indissoluble,[14] and that all sexual acts not undertaken to initiate the nurturing of children within the marital community deviate from the order of nature and are therefore vicious.[15] Thomas makes an exception of the sexual acts of married but infertile couples as well as involuntary sexual acts.[16] (He was, of course, not aware of the cyclic fertility of human females.) On the other hand, sexual acts are virtuous—good and meritorious—when ordered according to reason, which knows and presents the end of procreation. Unlike Augustine, Thomas does not see sexual desire as intrinsically suspicious. He distinguishes the sexual pleasure proportionate to sexual acts from concupiscence, disordered or irrational passion, and says that sexual acts, and not virginity only, can manifest the virtue of chastity,[17] if sexual desire and activity are directed toward procreation.

The pattern of Thomas's ethics conforms to the law of nature in that he derives moral norms from what humans are essentially and ought to strive to become. Essential human nature is distinguished by rationality and freedom, though it also includes characteristics shared with other animals, and even with vegetation and inanimate creatures. The fundamental source for Thomas's ethics is his reflective understanding of what "the human" or "human nature" comprises, not in an actual so much as in an ideal sense. What is it that is most *genuinely* human? he asks. It is in this that virtue consists, and against it that vice is defined. The ideally human, however, is a concept and standard at which one can arrive only through a process of observation and critical abstraction from what exists de facto. To this extent, the "abstract" method of natural law morality is necessarily empirical.[18]

Both Thomas and his latter-day interpreters must rely upon some sort of descriptive account, more or less formal, more or less methodical, more or less quantifiable, of the actual human situation. It is only in light of this situation and in contrast to it that it makes sense to define any ideal criterion of its evaluation. This fact has not always received the attention it deserves. I have in mind here, rather than Thomas himself, those of his commentators who assumed an excessively rationalistic approach to natural law morality and forgot what is to us a truism: reason does not operate in a cultural vacuum.[19] Thomas himself was more circumspect, remarking that it is at the most general levels of natural law insight that we have the most certainty, while "the more we descend to matters of detail, the more we encounter defects."[20] Thomas's own reserve in regard to his project has been extended by twentieth-century critics. Many doubt not only that human reason is a unitary faculty occupying a privileged vantage point of objectivity and omniscience, but even that its object, "nature," is an unchanging and universal order, established at the creation. James Gustafson's skepticism in pushing the point is not extraordinary:

> Nature itself develops, and human activity involves participation in nature in such a way that some aspects of it are altered. . . . The recourse that theological ethics takes to nature necessarily will be much more complex and ambiguous than the traditional natural law theory provided.[21]

The critique of the philosopher Mary Midgley is complementary; she challenges the very premise that "human nature" is a clear and distinct entity at even one historical moment, since the paradigmatic human faculties, rationality and language, are not without animal parallels.[22]

A particular problem in Thomas's use of the concept "nature" as normative is the role of physical nature in defining virtue. Although it is intellect, which knows the truth, and free will, which chooses the good, that Thomas labels uniquely human,[23] nevertheless there are some human activities whose criteria are the capacities and purposes of the human body, and these may be shared with nonhuman species. An example Thomas gives is sexual intercourse, which in all animals naturally results in the preservation of the species.[24] An issue not explicitly developed by Thomas is the degree to which distinctively human abilities and purposes might transform the significance of shared animal ones. For instance, might procreation, a physical goal of sex, be controlled legitimately by more specifically personal goals? This question has propelled the immense controversy over artificial contraception which has fragmented Roman Catholicism in the present century.[25]

In sexual and medical ethics in the Thomistic tradition, the rule of bodily nature has seemed to predominate, notwithstanding arguments that the integrity of physical functions, e.g., the reproductive process, should not be preserved at the expense of the human spirit or of important human relationships. Thomas sometimes indicates that physical functions must be realized in humans in ways that further peculiarly human moral obligations, but physical norms of nature lack systematic or consistent integration with rational and volitional ones. For instance, he offers that the begetting of offspring, common to all the animals, must be carried out by humans in circumstances that will allow the continued support of both parents, since both are necessary to the welfare of the human child.[26] Yet Thomas neglects the fully personal meaning of human sexuality when he decides that the "unnatural vices" must be the most serious among sexual sins, because they frustrate the biological design and end of venereal actions. He regards as less serious acts such as rape or incest, which are physically complete but which commit the injustice of disrespect for the dignity proper to human persons.

THOMAS'S USE OF
DESCRIPTIVE ACCOUNTS
OF THE HUMAN

In verifying the adequacy of his normative theory, Thomas relies on empirical descriptions of the human situation, though he obviously did not have available quantifiable "data" in the modern sense. Thomas is inclined to appropriate rather uncritically much of what Aristotle "observed," specifically, about human reproduction. He relies additionally on his own observation of human nature and relationships, and on many of what in the thirteenth century were assumed to be the "facts." Some of Thomas's well-known foibles are due to his appropriation of now obsolete biology, for example, his and Aristotle's attribution of femaleness to extrinsic influences on the male seed, his ideas about when "hominization" of the fetus occurs,[27] and his apparent notion that intercourse during menstruation can harm offspring.[28] The difficulty of separating "fact" from "value" is apparent in the definitions of such facts themselves, for their misconstruals of reality tend consistently to support the idea of female inferiority which was so thoroughly an assumption of the cultures of both Thomas and Aristotle. Thomas assumes a general consensus about the lesser rationality of the woman, her naturally subordinate place in the household and in society, and the superior wisdom and judgment of the man.

It must be said in Thomas's favor that his anthropology avoids dualism, for he consistently aligns the status of female rationality with that of female corporeality. A key point of evidence for the subordination of women in Thomas's world view is what he takes to be the "observed" inferiority of the female body, which he seems to associate causally with female inferiority of mind. The central piece of empirical data in this theory is what Thomas understands to be the nature of the reproductive process. He makes a good example both of the necessary dependence of the theologian on contributory disciplines, and of the peril of placing too serene a confidence in the conclusions of these other sciences. Like his contemporaries, Thomas thinks that "the seed of the man" is the "active principle" of human generation, which attracts and gives form to "the matter" supplied by the womb of the woman. The male creates a likeness of himself, much as the acorns of an oak tree grow up only into other oaks. Thus, "when the generation is completed, the seed itself, unchanged and fulfilled, is the offspring which is born."[29] The birth of a female can only be the result of a flaw in the reproductive process, so that the woman is, as Aristotle phrased it, "a misbegotten male."[30] This pejorative etiology is qualified somewhat by Thomas's views, referring to the Genesis creation accounts, that both male and female belong to the perfection of the species;[31] and that Eve, like Adam, was "formed immediately" by God, who made both out of some preexisting matter, "the slime of the earth," and a rib.[32]

Role differentiation is endorsed by Thomas as the natural concomitant of the biological differences between the sexes. Male and female are complementary and equal in that each is bound to do his or her part; however, as in the "marriage act," the "more noble part" belongs to the husband in "the household management, wherein the wife is ruled and the husband rules."[33] Although he thinks women are created to be subject to men, Thomas does allow that it is sin that distorts the naturally hierarchical relation into one that is exploitative on one side and "servile" on the other.[34] Eve is made from Adam's rib to symbolize that she is at his side in their "social union," neither exercising authority over him, nor yet his slave.[35] Thomas clearly holds that sexual differences will not be abolished in heaven, since they belong to the perfection of human nature, but sexual union for procreation will no longer be necessary.[36]

One commentator, Kari Elisabeth Børreson, has argued that although women are subordinate to men in history, in Thomas's scheme, they are equivalent to men after the resurrection. This is so because they share intellect and immortal souls, and, like men, are destined to enjoy the vision of God in whose image they were

made (even though that image is possessed by men more perfectly).[37]
Evidence in favor of Børreson's thesis is that Thomas tells us,

> Woman is subject to man on account of the frailty of nature, as
> regards both vigor of soul and strength of body. After the res-
> urrection, however, the difference in those points will be not on
> account of the difference of sex, but by reason of the difference
> of merits.[38]

Thomas appeals to the biblical account of the women who were the
first to see the risen Lord.

> Hereby, moreover, it is shown, so far as the state of glory is
> concerned, that the female sex shall suffer no hurt; but if women
> burn with greater charity, they shall also attain greater glory from
> the Divine vision: because the women whose love for our Lord
> was more persistent . . . were the first to see Him rising in
> Glory.[39]

This text is striking because it focuses on charity, love of God which
extends to those God loves, as the criterion for participation in the
divine vision. Men and women are equal in their capacity to receive
and express this supernaturally bestowed and most excellent virtue,
which surpasses both the natural intellectual and moral virtues, and
the other theological virtues, hope and faith.[40]

Thomas's view of the equality of women after the resurrection
becomes problematic if we consider the centrality of the intellect in
Thomas's definition of human nature,[41] and even of eternal happiness. We recall that Thomas denies full equality to the created
nature of woman. First, it is deficient in body, both because the
female body results from corruption of the male seed, and is generally passive, especially in the act of generation. More crucially,
the female nature is deficient in reason. In defining the last end of
the human person as the beatific vision, unending union with God,
Thomas argues that it is this alone that is proportionate to the natural
desire of the intellect to reach the First Cause of all created being,
and to enjoy "perfect happiness." The latter consists in "nothing
else than the vision of the Divine Essence."[42] In the *Summa Contra
Gentiles*, he says explicitly that "the ultimate felicity of man lies in
the contemplation of truth," and more precisely, "in the contemplation of God."[43] It is exactly in the area of intellect, however, that
women are inferior, and, while Thomas does deny that women will

be at a disadvantage after the resurrection, he nowhere asserts what would seem to be a prerequisite of their equality, namely, that their deficiency of reason will be compensated. He deflects the issue of disproportion between natural and supernatural status by protesting that differences in finite intellect are "practically nothing" compared to the infinite perfection of God, and shifts to the criterion of merit, charity, or "virtue" as the "road to felicity."[44] Although this move may represent an egalitarian impulse, it must be asked whether it fragments the person as a unity of body, intellect, will, and "soul."

Thomas, influenced by the Christian and biblical image of God's nondiscriminatory love, appears convinced that in matters of ultimate importance, men and women deserve equal consideration. His analysis of their natural status remains determined, however, by subordinationist elements, derived partly from philosophical and theological sources (Aristotle and Augustine), and partly from the medieval social milieu. As a consequence, the descriptive accounts of masculine and feminine with which he substantiates his theory of male and female nature remain skewed from the standpoint of the observer to favor the male.

When we turn from his general view of men and women to sexual ethics, we also find cultural and traditional influences in Thomas's evaluation of the fact that the production of offspring does seem to be one result for which the sexual act is aptly designed.[45] Thomas elevates procreation as the single most important criterion of morally right sexual activity, and relates this end to the welfare of the race rather than of the individual.[46] Of course, in both ancient Greece and medieval Europe, marriage and sexuality itself had functions that were more institutional, familial, and social than they were individual or "interpersonal" in the present affective and romantic sense. The indissolubility of marriage, for example, is linked by Thomas only on occasion to the complete commitment in love of the spouses. It is more centrally related to the needs of the species for the raising of offspring; of the family, especially the father, for certainty of lineage, and for harmonious familial relations; of civil society for services rendered via the institution of marriage; and to the benefits to the church inhering in the matrimonial sign of Christ's presence.[47]

Thomas downplays sexual pleasure and even the intimacy and love of the partners as motives for sexual expression, tolerating the former as a "venial sin," and speaking of the latter primarily in relation to the total project of married life. This is probably as it should be, but the importance of sexual intimacy as an expression and enhancement of the "friendship" of which Thomas speaks surely deserves more attention than he gives it.

To Thomas's credit, it must be said that his own good sense often qualifies his "data" and his theoretical preconceptions. Although polygamy might further the interest of the race in propagating itself, and could be supported by Old Testament examples, Thomas objects not only that it contravenes Christian teaching but also that it would reduce the "friendship of wife for husband" to a "servile relationship" (as is "corroborated by experience"), and that in a polygamous marriage "the friendship will not be equal on both sides."[48] He also speaks in a tone of appreciation, if not direct personal experience, when he insists that there is "the greatest friendship between husband and wife,"[49] and that the love of a man for his wife is the most "intense" of loves because "she is united with her husband, as one flesh."[50] Predictably, the argument is stated exclusively from the man's point of view. Aquinas's struggle with the available social and physical "facts," by the way, is instructive in regard to twentieth-century claims to possess "value-free" or "scientifically verifiable" data, and to all arguments that take the form "It is obvious that . . . ."

THOMAS'S USE OF CHURCH TRADITION: THEOLOGY AND PRACTICE

Aquinas's hermeneutical relation to his sources is made manifest further when we consider the reference point of Christian tradition. "Tradition" includes both the major theologians and teachers upon whom Thomas explicitly relies (e.g., Augustine and Peter Lombard) and the cumulative history of custom and church practice in thirteenth-century form. Augustine's enumeration of the three goods of marriage against the Manicheans, despite his ambivalence toward sex, established the shape of the theological tradition about marriage. Offspring, fidelity, and sacrament are cited by Thomas from the

Sentences of Peter Lombard, though he also quotes Augustine's *On the Good of Marriage*.[51] Augustine's paradigmatic assessment was that marriage's good consists in children, the faithfulness of the partners, specifically, the right of the spouses over one another's bodies,[52] and the indissoluble bond that symbolizes the union of Christ and church.[53] Augustine also acknowledges the companionship, mutual respect, and services that characterize the marriage bond, though he too sees virginity as a higher state. Augustine takes a more negative view of sex in marriage than does Aquinas, seeing it as inescapably tainted by concupiscence.[54] Although he declines to pronounce definitively on whether, if Adam and Eve had retained their original purity, God would have found "some other way" to continue the race,[55] Augustine does volunteer the judgment that "freedom from all sexual intercourse" is "an angelic ideal."[56] The acceptance of this teaching by Aquinas as normative tradition is modified by his greater appreciation for the friendship of the spouses and the intensification of their love by physical union. Thomas does not suggest that sexual intercourse would have been inappropriate for Adam and Eve, but only that their sexual passions always would have been ordered rightly.

BIBLICAL WARRANTS

We have already noted that Aquinas's assignment of a reproductive and domestic role to women, ostensibly because of their "nature," reflects the expectations of medieval society, as does their subjection to the patriarchal head of household. The status quo in church practice sometimes receives a similarly superficial foundation in "revelation." For instance, Thomas appeals to the biblical comparison of Christ and church to man and wife (Ephesians 5) to support the preconceived idea that, while second marriages are sacramental, there is a "defect" in the sacrament if the wife, but not the husband, has been married before. As he puts it, "though Christ has but one church for his spouse, there are many persons espoused to Him in the one church."[57]

In using biblical resources, of course, Thomas did not have the benefit of modern historical-critical tools which might have shed light upon the original meanings of texts. Nor did he share the modern hermeneutical concern to set each text in context, or to balance its interpretation by reference to the breadth of the canon. Although Thomas refers frequently to biblical texts, he employs almost as frequently a "proof text" method, in which citations are adduced to support conclusions at which he has arrived using the method of natural law.

Multiple examples could be given. Thomas infers from Matt. 5:32 that "our Lord" permitted divorce for "fornication," although not remarriage.[58] Scholars today, as we noted, do not generally take the Matthean version of the divorce prohibition as an authoritative saying of Jesus; nor do they by any means agree that the exception added by the evangelist refers to extramarital sex, or that when "divorce" is mentioned in the text it implies separation only. A prime example of interpretation to suit theological preconception is Thomas's attempt to explain out of existence the concubines of the patriarchs. "Wherever in the Old Testament we read of concubines being taken by such men as we ought to excuse from mortal sin, we must needs understand them to have been taken in marriage, and yet to have been called concubines. . . ."[59]

Thomas is fairly faithful to St. Paul's rationale in preferring virginity to marriage, though he liberally combines Paul with Aristotle. Marriage entails an unhappy "solicitude for temporal things" (1 Cor. 7:29)[60] and consequently less devotion to "the good of the soul."[61] Furthermore, he adds, sex diminishes reason[62] and detracts from "the good of the contemplative life."[63] Thomas reads St. Paul through Aristotle's eyes insofar as he freely translates the "undivided devotion to the Lord" of 1 Cor. 7:35 into the soul's own welfare. Paul's urgent and imminent eschatology is completely lost on Thomas, as it was on many in the tradition who failed to appreciate the radical difference of the New Testament world view to their own, or else disallowed in principle that Jesus or the inspired writers might have had mistaken impressions of the chronology of the last days. As a result they and Thomas pass on Paul's advice to the unmarried in abstraction from the communal context that gave it its original significance. Paul's specific preference may not, by the thirteenth century, meet his general communal criterion of adequate embodiment of Christ, or at least not meet it in the same way and for the same reasons. Yet Thomas bolsters Paul's preference for celibacy with an Aristotelian, and not particularly biblical, anthropology and "hands it on" in an aura of personal perfectionism rather than of communal service.

The Pauline criterion may be met more adequately by Thomas in his thesis that marriage is a sacrament. As such, it actually makes present in the community the reality that it signifies, that is, the presence of Christ in the church. This sacramental view of marriage also can be related to a shift in the Christian tradition from the imminent eschatology of the primitive church to an eschatology in which the kingdom is expected in the distant future, so that the stress falls on its present accessibility in the Christian community, through the Spirit.[64]

It no doubt would be a mistake to define "appropriate" interpretation of the Bible exclusively in relation to the sort of historical and sociological information about the original communities of authorship in which we are so interested today. Descriptions of the primitive church improve with the adequacy of the tools available to disclose it even though those tools are employed only with the help of certain presuppositions about the matter they are designed to study. It is, however, not as object of historical analysis but as authoritative canon; as narrative, story, and symbol system; as founding myth; that the Bible has been the continuing fount of Christian self-understanding. Its power to shape the body of Christ has not been contingent upon the availability of certain critical tools and empirically based methods of investigation. This is not to say that the best tools available at a certain time simply are dispensable. They can help the interpreter avoid unwitting or uncritical inconsistency with the fundamental import of a text or discover a sense of the text that is significant for both original and subsequent communities of interpretation. They also can align textual interpretations with central themes yielded by a writing or book within the canon, or by the canonical collection. It is clear, however, that the sensitivity of an interpreter to an issue or value within the Bible depends on the molding of the individual or group that uses the Bible as a resource. Interpretation proceeds on the basis of a "story" or self-understanding sustained by the community founded on the biblical accounts and maintained by constant reference to them. The communal ability to perceive and appropriate goes far beyond a "scientific" or "historically accurate" rendering of the meaning of texts to their original composers.

Something of the process, for good and ill, of the "handing on" of biblical texts within a tradition can be discerned in Thomas's use of the Genesis creation narratives in shaping his account of the differences and relations between men and women. On the one hand, Thomas intermixes citations from the two narratives and even from 1 Corinthians and Ephesians, without distinction of biblical context. On the other hand, he is quite consistent in using the biblical insights that the image of God characterizes all humanity, that sexual differentiation is good and complementary, and that it serves the purposes of procreation and social partnership. Thomas cites Genesis 2 to the effect that God made the first man out of "the slime of the earth" and the woman out of his rib, but associates the "breath of life" with the rational soul, thereby implying a body-soul distinction foreign to both Genesis 1 and 2. Thomas's further conclusion that it is the intellectual nature of humans in which inheres God's image seems to reflect more of Aristotle than of Genesis 2.[65] Thomas does insist that the body and soul were made together, since they together make up human nature.[66] Men and women both possess God's image, since both have a human mind, in which he tells us, in a statement inconsistent with his statements elsewhere that women are less rational, that "there is no sexual distinction."[67] As support, he adds, again out of context, the proclamation of Paul that "there is neither male nor female."

Thomas finally weighs the theory of lesser female body and intellect more heavily in the balance, for he believes that although both sexes possess the intellectual nature, and thus the image, the image in the man is superior to that in the woman. After all, the Apostle says "man is the beginning and the end of woman; as God is the beginning and end of every creature."[68] The purpose of the woman's creation is to provide a "helper" (Gen. 2:18) by which Thomas clearly means a subordinate. His view of the sort of help primarily intended by her creator resembles the view of the author of Genesis 1, if Phyllis Bird is right;[69] but not of the author of Genesis 2, from which Thomas takes the citation. She is to help in the task of procreation, and in the ancillary work of establishing a family and household.[70] Thomas does not cite Genesis 3 in describ-

ing woman's subordinate status. He disagrees with its possible implication that hierarchy itself intrudes through sin, supporting instead the presupposition of his theological and social traditions that
male primacy is "natural."

As noted earlier, Thomas associates the rib from which Eve was
taken with the cooperative "social union" of male and female, and
cites the "two in one flesh" and "cleaving" together of Gen. 2:24 in
support both of sexual procreative union[71] and of the domestic and
social partnership of a married couple,[72] including the intensity of
their love for one another.[73]

Thomas deviates not only from the text but from the eventual
theological consensus in his position that Eve's sin of pride was
greater than that of Adam, for "the woman was more grievously
punished than the man." Although Genesis 2 indeed portrays the
woman as the active sinner, as Thomas notices, the parallel punishments of Genesis 3 do not substantiate Thomas's excusing Adam
for having sinned passively "out of a certain friendly good will."[74]
In fact, the judgment of the Lord indicates that the complacent and
indolent follower in evil is just as guilty, not only of disobedience,
but of self-deception, as is the credulous and foolhardy leader.
Thomas does perceive the sinfulness inherent in the resulting distortion of the created order by male domination since he attributes
to sin the actual historical situation of the "servile" subjection of
woman.[75]

In sum, it is fair to say of Thomas that his basic source of normative ethics is a philosophical theory of natural law, derived
through a process of observation of the human reality as he knew
it. He imposed intelligibility on and assessed that reality by using
categories available through his own social, philosophical, and theological traditions. The Bible was influential in forming those traditions, since medieval European society and most intellectual disciplines were thoroughly Christian, at least in a cultural sense if not
in a radically biblical sense. Yet Thomas rarely approaches the biblical witness as a source with its own integrity, or allows it to challenge his world view, or to initiate rather than decorate his process
of theological reflection. If the thought of Thomas about men and
women, marriage, and sex does not always escape the strictures of
a medieval outlook, I think we hardly can regard his failure as greater

or more culpable than the idealization of individual freedom and glorification of sex, equally unbiblical, that often accompany the modern view of what is natural and fulfilling for humans. Thomas's strength lies in his dedication to painstaking reflection on experience and on his philosophical and theological sources. He organizes the results into a system of explanation with the persuasive force of reasonableness, internal coherence, and fidelity at some fundamental level to common human experience. His most valuable and original contribution to a Christian theology and ethics of sexuality is his insight that marital commitment is a profound form of friendship, intensified by physical expression. His definition of marriage as a "sacrament" also suggests that this sexually expressed union is a vehicle of Christ's presence in the community.

NOTES

1. Thomas Aquinas, *Commentary on Book III of the Sentences* 3.5.2.
2. ST I.92.1. Citations of Thomas are from the *Summa Theologica* (ST) unless otherwise indicated. The translation used is that by the Fathers of the English Dominican Province (New York: Benziger Brothers, 1948). The treatise on marriage found in the Supplement to the *Summa* is not the work of Thomas's own hand, but was compiled posthumously from Thomas's *Commentary on Book IV of the Sentences* of Peter Lombard. Citations from the *Summa Contra Gentiles* (SCG) are taken from the translations by Vernon J. Bourke (Book III) and Charles J. O'Neill (Book IV) (Notre Dame, Ind.: Univ. of Notre Dame Press, 1975).
3. ST I.92.1; cf. 2; II–II.156.1; Suppl. 64.5, SCG 3/II.123.
4. ST I.92.1.
5. ST Suppl.49.1.
6. ST II–II.152.4; SCG 3/II.125.6.
7. ST Suppl. 49.5, 6.
8. ST Suppl. 65.5.
9. ST Suppl. 49. esp. 3; 2167.1; ST II–II.153.2; SCG 3/II.123, 126.
10. ST II–II.26.11.
11. SCG 3/II.123.
12. ST Suppl. 41.1
13. Thomas, of course, differs from Aristotle by taking the position that it is preferable to remain a virgin than to engage in sexual activity at all (ST II–II.152.4).
14. SCG 123, 124. Marriage, though, is "holier" without "carnal intercourse," which is not necessary to constitute a marriage (Suppl. 42.4).
15. SCG 3/II.122; II–II.154.

16. ST II–II.154.5, 64.5 ad 3; SCG 3/II.122.5.

17. ST II–II.152.3 ad 5, 164.1; ST Suppl. 41.3,4; 49.4,5; SCG 3/II. 126–7.

18. Cf. James M. Gustafson, "Nature: Its Status in Theological Ethics," *Logos* 3 (1982): 9.

19. E.g., the authors of the Roman Catholic natural law moral "manuals" of the late nineteenth and early twentieth centuries.

20. ST I–II.94.4; cf.2.

21. Gustafson, "Nature," 21–22.

22. Mary Midgley, *Beast and Man: The Roots of Human Nature* (Ithaca, N.Y.: Cornell Univ. Press, 1978).

23. ST I–II.94.2.

24. ST I–II.94.2.

25. See Pope Paul VI's *Humanae Vitae* (1968), especially par. 14 and 17, in which he rejects the counterargument of the Majority Report of the Papal Commission on Birth Control. Thomas proscribes "every emission of semen" in any way from which "generation cannot follow" as "contrary to the good for man" (SCG 3/II.123.5; II–II.154.1).

26. ST Suppl. 41.1.

27. ST II–II.62.8; *Commentary on Book III of the Sentences* 3.5.2.

28. ST Suppl. 64.3.

29. SCG IV.45.

30. ST I.92.1 ob 1, ad 1.

31. ST I.91.1; SCG IV.88.

32. ST I.92.4.

33. ST Suppl. 64.5; cf. 41.1. So Thomas is an example of the subordinationist interpretations of Genesis which have so typified Christianity and contributed to its status as a patriarchal religion.

34. ST I.92.1.

35. ST I.92.3.

36. SCG IV.83, 88; ST Suppl. 81.4; cf. 79.2, 80.4.

37. Kari Elisabeth Børreson, *Subordination and Equivalence: The Nature and Role of Woman in Augustine and Thomas Aquinas* (Washington, D.C.: Univ. Press of America, 1981).

38. ST Suppl. 81.4.

39. ST III.55.3.

40. ST II–II.23.6.

41. In discussing the relation of body and soul, Thomas refers to the latter primarily in terms of human rationality, insisting that "the difference which constitutes man is *rational*, which is applied to man on account of his intellectual principle. Therefore the intellectual principle is the form of man" (ST I.76.1).

42. ST I–II.3.8; SCG 3/I.51, 48.

43. SCG 3/I.37.

44. SCG 3/I.58.

45. The incompleteness of Thomas's biological information did not permit him to note as morally significant the fact that the human female has a limited time of fertility, and that sexual union occurs in humans beyond that time. If he had been aware of the relative brevity of the fertile period, it might have suggested to him that the "design" of the act of sexual intercourse is ordered to ends beside procreation.

46. SCG 3/II.122–9.
47. ST Suppl. 49.3.
48. SCG 3/II.124; cf. ST Suppl. 65.1.
49. SCG 3/II.123.6.
50. ST II–II.26.11.
51. ST Suppl. 49.
52. *On the Good of Marriage* (OGM) 6–7. Augustine states, like Aquinas, that to seek sexual intercourse for pleasure is a venial sin, though the petitioned spouse has a duty to comply.
53. Cf. OGM 24.
54. OGM 13.
55. OGM 2.
56. OGM 8. See also *Against the Two Letters of the Pelagians* and *On Marriage and Concupiscence*. An excellent treatment of Augustine's views of sex, marriage, and sin is David F. Kelly, "Sexuality and Concupiscence in Augustine," *The Annual of the Society of Christian Ethics, 1983*, ed. Larry L. Rasmussen (The Society of Christian Ethics, distributed by the Council on the Study of Religion, Wilfrid Laurier University, Waterloo, Ontario), 81–116.
57. ST Suppl. 63.2 ad 2.
58. ST Suppl. 62.1,5.
59. ST Suppl. 65.5.
60. ST Suppl. 49.1
61. ST II–II.152.4.
62. Aristotle *Ethics* vii.11.
63. ST II–II.152.4; ST Suppl. 49.1.
64. I have addressed this possibility in "Sex, Marriage, and Community in Christian Ethics," *Thought* 58/228 (1983): 72–81.
65. On the difference between image and likeness, a traditional theological construal only superficially related to Gen. 1:26, see ST I.93.9.
66. ST I.91. Thomas moves toward dualism when he concludes that the immortal soul survives the death of the body in separation from it (ST I.76.1 ad 5, ad 2). Contrast this to the more biblical imagery of "resurrection life" or "resurrection of the body." Cf. Krister Stendahl, ed., *Immortality and Resurrection* (New York: Macmillan Co., 1965).
67. ST I.93.6 ad 2.
68. ST I.93.4 ad 1; cf. 1 Cor. 11:8–9.
69. See pp. 46–48 above.
70. ST I.92.1.

71. ST I.92.1.

72. ST I.92.2; SCG 3/II.124.7.

73. ST II–II.26.12. Thomas assumes that the male-female unity of Genesis is the equivalent of marriage, though neither Genesis account speaks of any formal institution of marriage. Following a particular theological and ecclesiastical agenda (and Augustine), i.e., to maintain the validity of the marriage of Mary and Joseph while retaining the doctrine of Mary's perpetual virginity, he also dissociates physical union from the essence of marriage. In contrast, Genesis 1 mentions procreation, and Genesis 2, without actually mentioning procreation, uses the term "one flesh," which Thomas interprets as sexual union for the purpose of procreation (cf. ST Suppl. 43.4; III.29.2).

74. ST II–II.163.4.

75. ST I.92 ad 2.

——— 7 ———

MARTIN LUTHER:
Marriage, Procreation, and *Sola Scriptura*

There is an interesting paradox in Martin Luther's thought about marriage which is well expressed in his treatise on *The Estate of Marriage* (1522).[1] This paradox will remind us not only of Luther's tendency to think in extremes, but also of the importance in his theology and ethics of a few persistent themes. These are the goodness of creation; the radical effects of sin; the essence of the Christian life as living in faith out of God's grace and righteousness, given to us in Christ; the central presence in the Christian's life of suffering through which he or she shares in the cross of Christ.

Luther begins *The Estate of Marriage* by examining the biblical foundations for a positive theology and ethics of marriage. He cites Gen. 1:27–28 to establish that God created two different sexes as part of his "divine and good creation," then commanded them to "come together in order to multiply." Sexuality and procreation, as well as the "estate of marriage" that institutionalizes them, are all part of a "divine ordinance," an "ordinance of creation." Sex and marriage are not merely optional, but are the word and command of God embodied in the natures of men and women. Only a few persons are exempt from this command to marry and procreate, either by physical circumstances or by the very rare gift of celibacy.[2]

Given this benevolent and biblical beginning, the last sentence of *The Estate of Marriage* is a text that perplexes one as much as Rom. 1:17 once perplexed Luther himself, spurring the reader to reread and ponder its sense.[3]

> Intercourse is never without sin; but God excuses it by his grace because the estate of marriage is his work, and he preserves in and through the sin all that good which he has implanted and blessed in marriage.[4]

This passage suggests some questions: Why is the sexual act always sinful, if it is part of God's ordinance and command? Is God a cosmic utilitarian who commands sin that good may result? How can God command a sinful act, then "excuse" it? Indeed, why is it in need of excuse if it is commanded and the avenue through which the promise of the creation is fulfilled? Is Luther by means of this paradox articulating a theologically coherent position? Or is it another instance of his notorious disinterest in systematic thought, as well as a remnant of an Augustinian and unbiblical negativity toward all sexual activity?

More confusingly, this example of a dim view of sex is not altogether anomalous in Luther's writings. In the *Lectures on Genesis* (1535–1536), he repeatedly refers to sexual desire and union as occasions of "shame" and "disgust."[5] At other points Luther assures us again that God overlooks the "impurity" of marriage because "it is done to bring forth children and God approves of this for it is his ordinance." In fact, "God will . . . build his kingdom of heaven over this work and cover up everything that is unclean in it."[6]

In an overview of Luther's work, we find that it is not only diffuse and full of ad hoc contentions but also that it is stimulated by biblical insights consistent with his principle of *sola Scriptura*. At the least Luther constantly turns back to scriptural evidence. Like Thomas, Luther repeats received tradition and qualifies it when it runs counter to life and human relationships as he understands them. Luther stands apart from Thomas, however, in his willingness to reconsider radically the premises of the Christianity of his day in the light of the Bible, and appears to read the Bible more critically than Thomas, looking at the context of a passage or at its Greek or Hebrew formulation in order to ascertain its full sense. This does not mean, of course, that his interpretation always measures up to modern critical standards.[7] Yet it does generate the fresh perspective that shapes Luther's critique of the late medieval Christian assignment of low status to sex and marriage, and its theoretical exaltation of clerical celibacy.

Luther's commentaries on Genesis and on 1 Corinthians 7 (1523) established important foundations for understanding his views of both marriage and the sexes who are united in marriage. In these works we find discoveries that are striking in their resemblance to modern efforts to bridge the gap the tradition has put between theology and the Scriptures by going back to the biblical texts. Luther's reflections on the event of sin in the Genesis creation stories, in particular, provide a key to the riddle: how can procreation and marriage be divinely mandated, and yet sexual intercourse can be, in fact always seems to be, sinful.

CREATION AND FALL

Luther first notices that humans are set apart from other creatures by God's deliberation and direct action, indicated by his statement, "Let us make" (Gen. 1:26).[8] The creation of Eve out of Adam's rib is no less miraculous nor immediately God's act than the creation of Adam out of a "clod" (cf. Trible, Jewett).[9] The purpose of sexual differentiation by the addition of a woman to the man is procreation for the good of the species. Luther interprets the blessing of increase as the reason Eve was made to be a "helper" (Gen. 2:18), for both sexes "are unable to procreate alone."[10] The process by which the work of procreation is accomplished is not only good and necessary in God's sight, but even "miraculous." Luther calls it "the lovely music of nature."

> Surely it is most worthy of wonder that a woman receives semen . . . which is given shape and nourished until the fetus is ready for breathing air. When the fetus has been brought into the world by birth, no new nourishment appears, but a new way and method: from the two breasts, as from a fountain, there flows milk by which the baby is nourished. All these developments afford the fullest occasion for wonderment and are wholly beyond our understanding.[11]

The creation of each child is no less marvelous than the creation of its original parents, and for this we should be grateful.

In the state of innocence in the Garden of Eden, not only procreation but also all physical functions, the raising of children, the provision of food, the gathering of sustenance from the natural environment, all forms of human cooperation, and even the transition from the physical to a spiritual life (death), would have been pure, delightful, congenial, and serene. Luther discourses at length and with enthusiasm on the fact that before the sin of Adam and Eve, the reason, the will, and the bodily sensations and capacities all reflected the image of God, and in a much more distinguished manner than after.[12] This original perfection included procreation and sexual intercourse. But, "in the state of innocence, Adam would not have known his Eve except in the most unembarrassed attitude toward God, with a will obedient to God, and without any evil thought."[13] Now, because of original sin, sex inevitably is accompanied by lust.[14] Yet concupiscence is not the intrinsic character of sex, nor does it eradicate its created goodness; "in itself, it's still licit and pure."[15]

Furthermore, the first pair was created to share equally in all their activities. Appealing to the similarity of the Hebrew words for "man" (ʾîš) and "woman" (ʾiššâ), Luther claims that Eve might be called "'she-man' from man, a heroic woman, who performs manly acts."[16] Luther, obviously, accepts the presupposition that the standard of excellent humanity is "man," but still moves beyond the conclusion that woman is intrinsically inferior. At her creation, he says, Eve was "the equal of Adam in all respects," and "in no respect inferior to Adam, whether you count the qualities of the body or those of the mind."[17] To call Eve a "maimed man" as did Aristotle is, in Luther's opinion, to ridicule the handiwork of God. Of Eve's "fellowship" with Adam, Luther adds, "Their partnership involves not only their means but children, food, bed, and dwelling; their purposes, too, are the same." Indeed, "Whatever the man has in the home and is, this the woman has and is."[18]

In believing the serpent and sharing the forbidden fruit, for the sake of which they disobeyed God and were cast out of Paradise, male and female also are equal. Both evade God's accusation and try to excuse their sin.[19] After sin, judgment is pronounced. The harmony of life is disrupted. Henceforth, human activities, including sexual and procreative ones, shall be carried out in exertion, suffering, conflict, and shame. Even the earth is cursed. Adam's labor and toil against it will be a burden that abates not, but becomes "far more difficult" with each generation. The husband's work of "supporting, defending, and ruling his own," and of participating in the instruction and governance of family, society, and church, "cannot be carried on without the utmost difficulties."[20] Eve, on the other hand, no longer has an equal share in these projects of human society; she has other burdens which are her own. One is the pain of childbirth and the labor of caring for children. She also suffers from the subjection to her husband which is sin's result and a devolution of her original equality with him. Now "Eve has been placed under the power of her husband, she who previously was very free and, as the sharer of all the gifts of God, was in no respect inferior to her husband." Luther reminds us that "if Eve had persisted in the truth, she would not only not have been subjected to the rule of her husband, but she herself would also have been a partner in the rule which is now entirely the concern of males."[21] In a mood that is at once pragmatic, critical, and humorous, Luther evaluates the present situation of female subordination:

> Women are generally disinclined to put up with this burden and they naturally seek to gain what they have lost through sin. If they are unable to do more, they at least indicate their impatience by grumbling. However, they cannot perform the functions of men, teach, rule, etc. In procreation and in feeding and nurturing their offspring they are masters. . . . On the woman obedience to her husband was imposed, but how difficult it is to bring this very condition about![22]

An indication of Adam's power over Eve is his naming her just as he did the animals, of which we are reminded, Luther tells us, "even today" by the customs by which a married woman adopts her husband's name and assumes his place of residence. These are "traces" of "sin" and "misfortune."[23] Luther also notes, as have modern commentators,[24] that the Genesis account is framed by the mention of nakedness, which at first was "commendable and delightful"[25] and later became shameful, "for through sin nature has lost its confidence in God."[26] Even after the fall, however, suffering, lust, and subjection are not simply to be accepted in resignation. The lost ideal furnishes a critical norm. "For if a wife is honorable, virtuous, and pious, she shares in all the cares, endeavors, duties, and functions of her husband."[27] The relations between men and women are not wholly poisoned; indeed, "There is no sweeter union than that in a good marriage."[28]

MARRIAGE

As we have seen, Luther views marriage as a "holy estate and divine ordinance," a "vocation" or "station," through which God orders human life.[29] Although marriage is a natural institution rather than a sacrament, as it had been for the medieval church, and though within the fallen creation it shares the impurity and sinfulness of other human activities and callings, Luther calls marriage "religious" if done in "the spirit of faith," for it causes us to "exercise trust in the Lord." Further, it "strengthens . . . the body outwardly through works; so that marriage promotes both faith and works and helps, supplies and guides both body and soul."[30] In the state of sin, marriage not only fulfills the natural duty of procreation, but also is an antidote to the sins of lust and eventual fornication,[31] and provides companionship and mutual support in the labors and burdens of life.[32] As Luther phrases it, quaintly and a bit condescendingly, but not without self-mockery, "The management of the household must have the ministration of the dear ladies."[33]

Luther's view of the present state of male-female relations and of marital association reflects not only his understanding of the disastrous effects of sin on God's good creation but also that of our sharing in the fruits of the redeeming work of Christ by sharing in his cross. The "theology of the cross" is contrasted by Luther to the false "theology of glory" of the "papists," and is perhaps as central to his reform of theology and of religious experience as is justification by faith. In the perspective of the cross, the difficulty, misfortune, illness, and loss of this life are "chastisements" sent by our gracious Father so that we might through his discipline be reconciled to him.[34] Suffering for Luther, even redemptive suffering, is never mystical, ethereal, or romantic; it is quotidian, practical, concrete, even trivial. In *The Order of Marriage for Common Pastors*, Luther sets forth an outline of the nature and purpose of marriage, and ties it to biblical texts, particularly from Genesis 1—3, Matthew 19, and Ephesians 5. Therein he refers to the verdicts of Genesis 3 as "the cross which God has placed upon this estate."[35] The division of gender roles that results is not merely a punishment, but also an avenue of reunion with God, if carried out in faith and trust in God and in gratitude for the blessings of creation and salvation. The wisdom of the world rejects the trivial cares and tasks of marriage and parenthood, since reason, as always, leads us astray when it pronounces on the ultimate importance of what it considers.[36] Luther felicitously expresses this elevated theological judgment in earthy, common-sensical terms:

> Now observe that when that clever harlot, our natural reason . . . takes a look at married life, she turns up her nose and says, "Alas, must I rock the baby, wash its diapers, make its bed, smell its stench, stay up nights with it, take care of it when it cries, heal its rashes and sores, and on top of that care for my wife, provide for her, labor at my trade, take care of this and take care of that, do this and do that, endure this and endure that, and whatever else of bitterness and drudgery married life involves?"
>
> Now you tell me, when a father goes ahead and washes diapers or performs some other mean task for his child, and someone ridicules him as an effeminate fool—though that father is acting . . . in Christian faith—my dear fellow you tell me, which of the two is most keenly ridiculing the other: God, with all his angels and creatures, is smiling—not because that father is washing diapers, but because he is doing so in Christian faith.[37]

What is done in the spirit of faith and trust and gratitude to God, even the most daily and ordinary sufferings and tasks, is pleasing to God and glorifies his name and work.

Luther, having seen its demands firsthand, also waxes eloquent on the "honor of motherhood," through which a woman not only serves God, but also retains some of the grandeur that was Eve's.[38] Although a woman may "suffer and even die" in childbirth, just as for the man "labors in the state and church wear out the body and drain off all vitality," the woman sacrifices "gloriously."[39] In short, I contend that Luther does not so declaim merely to "keep woman in her place," that is, out of the spheres of public influence that belong properly to men. It is true that Luther sees the division between these spheres and the domestic one as inevitable in the present order of things, and so does not call for or anticipate social reform that will close it. At the same time, he does not describe the division as characterized by the normativity that belongs to the order of nature.[40] The ideal for men and women is cooperation and shared authority, and his frank comments about marriage as he has experienced or seen it are most appreciative when describing relationships in which responsibility in many realms is shared. Women bear children and most expertly raise them, but even beyond the garden that is not their only contribution:

> Imagine what it would be like without this sex [woman]. The home, cities, economic life, and government would virtually disappear. Men can't do without women. Even if it were possible for men to beget and bear children, they still couldn't do without women.[41]

It is, however, simply a fact of life as Luther observes it that women, by and large, are not formally influential in the economic and political spheres. What he sees and recognizes is the female sex competently and perseveringly undertaking to raise families and manage households. His appreciation of the attributes and roles that he associates de facto with women is expressed in his image of God as one who "graciously cares for us like a kind and loving mother."[42]

Despite Luther's positive view of women as originally equal to men, some decided "sexist" implications of his theory cannot be overlooked. Luther basically accepts the subordination of women as "the ways things are now," even though not the ideal. Further, though he does praise motherhood, his exaltation of it as a "cross" by which to glorify God could be read as an endorsement of an attitude of passive resignation on the part of women who suffer real injustices in the domestic sphere. To be fair to Luther, he does make similar recommendations for the husband and father.

CELIBACY

Luther has much to say and little that is complimentary about celibacy.[43] He never rejects it completely in favor of marriage; in fact, he refers to it as a "greater gift."[44] He warns repeatedly, however, that this gift is not given frequently. Those who remain unmarried without it will be ensnared by lust and will fall into pollution and fornication, a common scourge of the clergy and monasteries. Compared to that of the married, the spiritual lives of most monks and nuns, he claims, are "wretched," "un-Christian, vain, and pernicious."[45] Although the existence of the clergy is one of comparative material ease, while that of those striving to support families is one of "outward bitterness," still marriage is an estate "pleasing" and "precious" to God.[46] Luther's sermon at the wedding of a cleric,

Sigismund von Lindenau, who was marrying publicly after seven years of secret marriage, contains pejorative comparisons of vowed celibacy to marriage throughout.[47]

Luther's commentary on 1 Corinthians 7 is dedicated as a "wedding present" to the marshal of the elector of Saxony. In it he counters the traditional interpretation of the chapter, which concluded that marriage is inferior to celibacy. This is one occasion on which Luther's own reformative inclinations distort the biblical evidence. He claims inaccurately that the historical setting of 1 Corinthians is the complete rejection of celibacy by Jewish Christians of Corinth, to whom Paul is responding in justifying celibacy. He also asserts (less forgivably, since his sense contravenes the clear tenor of the text) that the language and argument of 1 Corinthians 7 show Paul speaking "shyly" and "carefully" about the very permissibility of celibacy. According to Luther, Paul's high regard for marriage is obvious from the fact that he "persists in bringing in the state of matrimony."[48] Although Luther concedes that genuine celibacy is even more "beautiful, delightful, and noble" than marriage, indeed a "gift from heaven," it should not be forced on young people. Whoever does not have the ability to remain chaste "is commanded to marry," as if "from God" himself.[49]

DIVORCE

Luther's teaching on divorce is motivated by the same pastoral interest in the human situation as his teaching on celibacy. Generally speaking, Luther is not concerned to elaborate precise schemata of moral rules. He is content with the singular but comprehensive exhortation to live out of faith and serve one's neighbor. Most of Luther's examples of the moral life are occasioned by specific cases brought to him by the faithful or problem areas in popular or ecclesiastical practice.[50] Luther takes the estate of marriage to be accompanied by a natural inseparability,[51] but is willing to make accommodations when the action of one spouse makes a marriage intolerable for the other. Circumstances of this sort are adultery, desertion,[52] the refusal of the conjugal duty,[53] and coercion into an "un-Christian way of life."[54]

Luther cites the words attributed to Jesus in Matt. 19:3–9 in support of his position that the one who divorces an adulterous spouse is justified and may remarry.[55] He takes Paul's saying "from the Lord" in 1 Cor. 7:10–11 to mean that separation on grounds of incompatibility is allowable only if it is not followed by remarriage.[56] However, if a person is denied a reconciliation by an estranged spouse, and does not have the ability to remain celibate, then he or she may remarry, since "God will not demand the impossible."[57] In all of the above conditions, the civil authorities, to whose jurisdiction marriage belongs, should permit the dissolution of a marriage.

However, even though marriage is part of the created order, and belongs to the earthly or temporal kingdom, it is also a vocation in which the Christian can live out of his or her faith. States in life—marriage, ministry—are not sacramental for Luther, since the whole of the life of every true Christian will be an occasion of Christ's presence in the world. The only authentic sacraments are those that transform the whole life of the Christian as such by uniting it with Christ—Baptism and Eucharist. The Christian's life is in every respect "lived out of heavenly righteousness into the world."[58] It stands to be transformed in its entirety by "the evangelical call," "the call of the Gospel." The demand of this call is the loving service to the neighbor which belongs to faith: "All things are free to you with God through faith; but with men you are the servant of every man through love."[59] A true Christian will love and serve the neighbor even at the cost of his or her own interests and welfare, and will do so even in his or her marriage commitment. The person genuinely living under "the spiritual government" will not seek a divorce, even from a spouse whose conduct is reprehensible.[60] If one can "endure" the situation with "Christian fortitude" it will be "a wonderfully blessed cross and a right way to heaven."[61]

Luther, while rejecting the idea that marriage is a sacrament, and that it is thus an intrinsically unbreakable bond, still insists that true Christians will not seek to dissolve their marriages. Indissolubility is not connected with the state of marriage, but dissolution of marriage is inconsistent with the forbearance and self-sacrifice entailed by genuine Christianity. Luther moves the "sacramental" character of marriage, its ability to make present the reality of the fidelity and love that Christ shows toward the church, from the realm of an external status or institution to that of the Christian's personal existence in faith and bestowed righteousness.[62] For Luther, married Christians are not perfect individuals constrained by a perfectionist law. They are perfect individuals, *to the extent that* their Christianity is genuine. To that extent, they have no need of the law to guarantee that they will live out of faith and love.

SUMMARY

Luther's views of gender, of sexuality, and of marriage have their foundations in the Bible, particularly in the Genesis creation narratives. While the Pauline letters are important to him on other theological fronts, they are less so in this area, for he does not share, and indeed misinterprets, Paul's preference for virginity. For Luther, male and female complementarity and partnership, especially in carrying out the blessing of procreation, are established and mandated at the creation. Human relationships are but remnants and dregs of the original harmony of man and woman which, even so, they reveal as prototype and ideal.

Luther does seem of two minds about sex. Sexual passion, with what he perceives as its near irresistibility, appears always sullied by lust. Still, he marvels at the miracles of pregnancy and birth, extolls the maternal labors that nourish offspring, enjoins participation by the father, and speaks freely and affectionately of wife and children. Finally, he concedes to women at least a shade of the joint authority in human affairs that the Creator first intended them to inherit from Eve. Both in his theological writings and in the snippets of informal dialogue which his friends and followers so diligently recorded, we watch Luther struggle between anxiety about and even fear of sex *and* gratitude for the family made possible by sexual union and joined to him in the institution of marriage. We find a man unafraid to challenge the presuppositions of received traditions, to return to sources, and to re-create both religious foundations and the meanings of human existence that they undergird and enhance. Luther's ethics is empirical in the most immediate sense: he constantly tests Christian theory and practice by their adequacy to transform the brokenness, pain, and even tedium of daily affairs. His norm is an experience of faith fruitful in humility, piety, forgiveness, and works of love. Luther's unsystematic but straightforward and homey table conversations afford rare insight into the pastor, reformer, husband, and father in whose experience are united the contraries of sin and grace, reason and faith, merit and service, anger and tolerance, lust and love. Surely we smile at the recognition of ourselves when we hear him offer musingly a retrospective evaluation of a state of life that he not only observed and analyzed, but also experienced:

> When one looks back upon it, marriage isn't so bad as when one looks forward to it . . . . When I look beside myself, I see my brothers and sisters and friends, and I find that there's nothing but godliness in marriage. To be sure, when I consider marriage, only the flesh seems to be there. Yet my father must have slept with my mother and made love to her, and they were nevertheless godly people. All the patriarchs and prophets did likewise. The longing of a man for a woman is God's creation—that is to say, when nature's sound, not when it's corrupted as it is among Italians and Turks.[63]

Here, with prejudice and tolerance, scrupulosity and magnanimity, we have the typical, paradoxical, engaging Luther.

NOTES

1. Unless otherwise indicated, citations of Luther's writings will be from the American edition, *Luther's Works* (LW), vols. 1–30 (St. Louis: Concordia Pub. House); vols. 31–55 (Philadelphia: Fortress Press).

2. *The Estate of Marriage*, LW 45, 17–21.

3. In the *Table Talk* (1531–1544), there are two accounts of the "tower experience" in which Luther, in meditating on Rom. 1:17, came to realize that the "righteousness of God" is that by which he mercifully justifies the sinner, rather than that by which he punishes (LW 54, 193–94, 308–9).

4. *Estate of Marriage*, LW 45, 49.

5. *Lectures on Genesis*, LW 1, 62–3, 71, 105, 117, 118, 142.

6. *Sermon at the Marriage of Sigismund von Lindenau* (1545), LW 51, 365. In a similar vein, Luther prays, "Dear God . . . let us remain in the holy estate of matrimony, where thou dost wink at our infirmity" (*Table Talk*, LW 54, 295).

7. An example is his argument that 1 Corinthians 7 is addressed to Jews who see marriage as obligatory and that the "present distress" to which Paul refers is persecution of Christians (*Commentary on 1 Corinthians 7*, LW 28, 9, 49).

8. *Lectures on Genesis*, LW 1, 56.

9. Ibid., 123. Both Phyllis Trible, *God and the Rhetoric of Sexuality* (Philadelphia: Fortress Press, 1978), and Paul K. Jewett, *Man as Male and Female*

(Grand Rapids: Wm. B. Eerdmans, 1978) mention that God acts directly in creating both Adam and Eve. See above, pp. 54–55.

10. *Lectures on Genesis*, LW 1, 118, cf. 120–21 and *Marriage of Sigismund von Lindenau*, LW 51, 360. Although Luther associates procreation as the primary purpose of sexual difference with Genesis 2, Phyllis Bird and others have argued that Genesis 2 lends itself more readily to an interpretation in terms of partnership in other spheres than does Genesis 1, in which procreation is the only purpose for the creation of the woman (see above 46–48, 51).

11. *Lectures on Genesis*, LW 1, 126.

12. Ibid., 102–3; cf. 65, 86, 104, 119.

13. Ibid., LW 1, 62.

14. Ibid., 71, 104–5, 119, 142.

15. *Table Talk*, LW 54, 324; cf. 218.

16. Ibid., 137.

17. Ibid., 115.

18. Ibid., 137. On this score, however, as on some others, Luther was not wholly unambivalent. In his remarks on Gen. 1:27, he states that though Eve was "extraordinary," "she was nevertheless a woman," and "was not the equal of the male in glory and prestige." In the following paragraph, he wavers, saying that though the female sex is "inferior," it "may not be excluded from any glory of the human creature" (p. 69). He also follows a traditional interpretation of the fall when he argues that the serpent approached Eve because she was "weaker," since "in the perfect nature the male somewhat excelled the female" (p. 151). I think it fair to say that, on the whole, these qualified reaffirmations of the traditional view of Eve are outweighed by the passages in which Luther speaks in no uncertain terms of the original equality of man and woman. Perhaps Luther has such inconsistencies in mind when he protests that the lectures on Genesis were "hastily thrown together and are imperfect" (*Table Talk*, LW 54, 288–89)!

19. Ibid., 177–82.

20. Ibid., 211, 210, 204, respectively.

21. *Lectures on Genesis*, LW 1, 202–3. Luther explains that, in Paradise, "the management would have been equally divided," but "now the sweat of the face is imposed upon man, and woman is given the command that she should be under her husband" (p. 138).

22. Ibid., 203.

23. Ibid., 219.

24. For example, Trible, *God and the Rhetoric of Sexuality*, 116–19, 134.

25. *Genesis*, LW 1, 139.

26. Ibid., 167.

27. Ibid., 137.

28. *Table Talk*, LW 54, 33; cf. 223.

29. *Marriage of Sigismund von Lindenau*, LW 51, 358, 362–63; *The Order of Marriage for Common Pastors*, LW 53, 110, 111, 112; *Commentary on 1 Corinthians 7*, LW 28, 17–18, 20; LW 45, 17–18, 37–38.

30. *Commentary on 1 Corinthians 7*, LW 28, 17–18, 20.

31. In his early *Sermon on the Estate of Marriage* (1519), Luther calls marriage a "hospital for incurables" (LW 44, 9). In the same piece is found a statement that companionship, not procreation only, is part of the *natural* institution of marriage (p. 8).

32. With good-humored irony, Luther remarked at table that the "pleasantest" life, consisting in a "moderate household" and an "obedient wife," had yet to be arranged for him by God (*Table Talk*, LW 54, 218).

33. *Lectures on Genesis*, LW 1, 116; cf. 120–1.

34. Lennart Pinomaa, *Faith Victorious: An Introduction to Luther's Theology* (Philadelphia: Fortress Press, 1963), 3–5. Luther's theology of the cross is discussed in relation to his spirituality in a paper by John Todd, "An Everyday Theology," delivered to the Boston College-Andover Newton Theological School Doctoral Colloquium, Newton Centre, Mass., 3 December 1982.

35. *The Order of Marriage for Common Pastors*, LW 53, 114; cf. *Genesis*, LW 1, 201: the female "punishments" assigned in Genesis 3 are referred to as a "cross."

36. *The Estate of Marriage*, LW 45, 39–40.

37. See Brian A. Gerrish, *Faith and Reason: A Study in the Theology of Luther* (Chicago: Univ. of Chicago Press, Midway Reprint, 1979). Gerrish develops the argument that Luther does not reject reason wholly, but only its competence to address humanity's true relation to God.

38. *Genesis*, LW 1, 203. See Luther's comments on Adam's naming the woman Eve "because she is the mother of all the living." Luther calls this "a very pleasing and delightful name" in its significance (*Genesis*, LW 1, 219; cf. *Table Talk*, LW 54, 223).

39. Ibid., 213, 40, 213, respectively. Luther puts to theological use his experience and that of his wife as expectant parents in describing "Eve's sorrows": "The threat is directed particularly at birth and conception. But conception designates the entire time during which the fetus, after being conceived, is carried in the womb, a time beset with severe and sundry ailments. From the beginning of that time a woman suffers very painful headaches, dizziness, nausea, difficult vomiting, toothache, and a stomach disorder which produces a craving called pica, for such foods from which nature normally shrinks. Moreover, when the fetus has matured and birth is imminent, there follows the most awful distress, because only with the utmost peril and almost at the cost of her life does she give birth to her offspring. . . . Through marriage the husband transfers, as it were, a part of those punishments upon himself (for he cannot without grief see those things in his wife)" (*Lectures on Genesis*, LW 1, 200–201).

40. In an apparently off-the-cuff and, I hope, humorous remark, Luther makes an association between the differences of physical reproductive function and natural differences in domestic and public roles: "Men have broad shoulders and narrow hips, and accordingly they possess intelligence. Women have narrow shoulders and broad hips. Women ought to stay at home; the way they were created indicates this, for they have broad hips and a wide fundament to sit upon (keep house and bear and raise children)" (*Table Talk*, LW 54, 8).

41. Ibid., 161.

42. *Estate of Marriage*, LW 54, 43.

43. *The Judgment of Martin Luther on Monastic Vows*, LW 44, 243–400.

44. *Lectures on Genesis*, LW 1, 135.

45. *Estate of Marriage*, LW 45, 41, 42, respectively.

46. Ibid., 42.

47. *Marriage of Sigismund von Lindenau*, LW 51, 357–67.

48. *Commentary on 1 Corinthians 7*, LW 28, 9.

49. Ibid., 26.

50. See, for example, *On Marriage Matters* (1530), LW 46, 265–320. Therein he discusses the problems of secret engagements, which were common in his time; and of "impediments" to marriage, which had proliferated as a means of increasing revenue for the church via the granting of dispensations; as well as of divorce. Impediments also are discussed in *The Estate of Marriage*, LW 45, 17–49; and in *The Babylonian Captivity of the Church*, LW 36, 96–106.

51. *Lectures on Genesis*, LW 1, 138.

52. *Estate of Marriage*, LW 45, 30–35; *Table Talk*, LW 54, 302–49; *Commentary on 1 Corinthians 7*, LW 28, 36–38; *Babylonian Captivity*, LW 36, 106. Luther understands authority over marriage and divorce to belong to the state, not the church, and even calls for the death penalty for the adulterer (LW 45, 33).

53. *Estate of Marriage*, LW 45, 33–35. Luther thinks it just that the wife of an impotent husband demand his permission to beget heirs in a secret marriage to another, and vice versa (pp. 20–21); but maintains that a husband may not take another if his wife is an invalid and incapable of sexual intercourse. This burden is another "gift of grace" by which to serve God (p. 35). Cf. *Babylonian Captivity*, LW 36, 103–5.

54. *Commentary on 1 Corinthians 7*, LW 28, 36.

55. *Estate of Marriage*, LW 45, 30–31.

56. Ibid., 34; *Commentary on 1 Corinthians 7*, LW 28, 32.

57. *Commentary on 1 Corinthians 7*, LW 28, 32.

58. F. Edward Cranz, "Martin Luther," in *Reformers in Profile*, ed. B. A. Gerrish (Philadelphia: Fortress Press, 1970), 105.

59. *Commentary on 1 Corinthians 7*, LW 28, 46–47. Cf. Luther's *On Christian Liberty* (1520): "A Christian is a perfectly free lord of all, subject to none. A Christian is a perfectly dutiful servant of all, subject to all."

60. *Estate of Marriage*, LW 45, 31.

61. Ibid., 34.

62. In *The Babylonian Captivity of the Church* Luther objects that marriage is not somehow "sacred" simply because it takes place between believers. "Besides, even among believers there are married folk who are wicked and worse than any heathen; why should marriage be called a sacrament in their case and not among the heathen?" (LW 36, 93).

63. *Table Talk*, LW 54, 161.

─── 8 ───

THE ETHICS
OF SEXUALITY
in Christian
Perspective

Until the recent past, the primary framework in the Christian tradition for the evaluation of sexual acts and relations has been a communal one.[1] One of the reasons procreation has been connected so integrally with the moral significance of sex is that it is a form of service to the species and to particular civil and religious communities. Even the love and fidelity of spouses has been understood to serve the formation and preservation of a domestic unit apt for the nurture of young and contribution to larger societies of family, nation or tribe, and church. This social dimension of sexual ethics is evident in Augustine's articulation of marriage's three goods; in Aquinas's evaluation of marriage in terms of propagation and domestic partnership, and even in his definition of the sacramental character of marriage as a contribution to the church; and in Luther's naming marriage an "ordinance" serving God and creation. For all, the cooperation of man and woman is mandated for the fulfillment of these social ends, and to them the roles of the sexes also are ordained.

Biblical resources bear out this general perspective. Certainly the differentiation and union of the sexes in Genesis have as their context God's providence for the creation. Paul interprets all sexual relationship and his own preference for celibacy by the criterion of communal upbuilding to which he assumes the Christian will be devoted. Since love, commitment, and friendship between spouses are perceived by biblical and traditional authors as ancillary goods, sexual relations for their sake alone are seen as misdirected. It is this conclusion that the modern temperament judges a misrepresentation of human sexual experience and of the essential character of sexuality.

The discrepancy between the traditional, more biblical view of sexual morality, and the present Western one becomes more intelligible when the social and philosophical settings of each are cast in relief; every sexual ethics presupposes a social vision of some sort, which accounts, at least in part, for the coloring sexuality receives. A dominant stream of Western moral philosophy since the Enlightenment stresses the rationality, freedom, and autonomy of the individual; it is exemplified by the post-Lockean liberalism that has been so influential in North American mores and political life. In the liberal view, the autonomous adult exists to fulfill independently his or her own interests and needs, and is limited in attempts to do so only by the parallel and sometimes competing rights of others to do likewise. But individual autonomy has not always been prized so highly.

In the classical Greek (Athenian) view, for instance, "society" means primarily the aristocratic association of equals (free adult. males), and exists to further the virtuous and happy life led by the good citizen. Sexual relations in marriage serve the welfare and continuity of family and political communities. It is not unusual for the bonds of *eros* and *philia* to be fulfilled outside the community of spouses, in relations between males, since females are their inferiors. In the social vision of medieval Christianity, communities as well as persons are hierarchically related, with the church of more ultimate importance than the state. The woman obeys the authority of the man, and sexual "nature," which serves the species, is to be subordinated to higher, religious ends, realized most completely in the ideal of virginity. But in the view of Immanuel Kant, influential in modern philosophy, the community of surpassing importance is that of persons as "ends in themselves," an absolute respect for the dignity of whom defines moral obligation. While Kant went so far as to say that sexual desire by definition degrades the one to whom it is directed by making him or her a mere "object," neo-Kantian moral philosophy asserts in regard to sexuality that moral obligations are met if the freedom and rights of participants are respected. In the political and moral liberalism of the American constitutional tradition, John Locke's autonomy of the individual, Kant's "respect for person," and the existentialist philosopher's absolutization of choice, have been synthesized in an overriding emphasis on individual liberty and self-determination, which community exists in order to serve. Liberalism tends to support the moral, not merely legal, legitimacy of any liasons, sexual or otherwise, between consenting adults, so long as they do not harm others. An emphasis neglected by liberalism is the communal nature of the person that is manifested in the strong traditional stress on procreation as the primary contribution of the sexuality of the couple.

To the extent that Christian sexual ethics has followed philosophical examples, it has permitted procreation gradually to cede primacy of place to the interpersonal aspects of sexuality which were implicit but neglected in the Bible and tradition. A sexual act may or may not be procreative, but it is always an avenue of personal communication, and a constituent of the most intense and intimate human relationships possible. Passionate sexual love is not only to be controlled but affirmed; not only to be of service, but enjoyed. Affective relationship and personal satisfaction increasingly have tended to become necessary and sufficient criteria of sexual, marital, and even familial morality; while procreation is viewed as a merely incidental outcome of an interaction directed centrally and properly to the mutual gratification of the couple.[2] Reactions against extremes are liable to manifestation in parallel extremes; sexual ethics is not exceptional. But sexual ethics also proves the rule that the mean between extremes is precious. The negative or ambivalent attitudes toward sex which entailed that procreation be sex's justification, and which characterized most of traditional Christianity, surely are inadequate. Still, liberal individualism and relativism in sexual ethics stand to be corrected by the traditional service-oriented and communal ideals against which contemporary personalism arose as a modification.

Among the social visions of the Bible, we encounter the Israelite "covenant people" of Yahweh, Jesus' "kingdom of God," and Paul's "body of Christ." These are all strikingly corporate images of society. In the New Testament, the individual increases in importance through the universality and inclusivity of the gospel. Membership in the community depends on repentance and conversion, from which no person is in principle excluded. Community is affirmed in a manner that entails rather than denigrates the value of the person. In the correlative sexual ethics, sexual acts express conversion to or alienation from the community; this is especially true in the New Testament, where any legalistic approach to sexual morality is abandoned *without* abandonment of the idea that the moral lives of individuals do make a difference to the life of the community as a whole, and their inclusion in it.

The relatively narrow perspective of modern Western moral philosophy also is contested by anthropological and cross-cultural comparisons. This is not to say that fulfillment of the sexual couple, and the depth of the relationship to which they give sexual expression, is of negligible importance, or even an inappropriate focus for Christian sexual ethics. It does imply, however, that the submergence of the communal by the interpersonal represents a distinct departure, not only from biblical and Christian views of marriage but also from those that have undergirded the institutionalization of sexuality in most human societies. Many Western and non-Western and modern and primitive cultures have construed the social significance of sexuality not just in terms of the socially contributory partnership of any two individuals whose cooperative relation is expressed and cemented by sexual expression, but specifically in terms of the biological families that function as interlocking and self-perpetuating units of society.

The emphasis on community, especially as it appears in the New Testament, also provides a vision of the moral life in which it is possible to get beyond Christianity's traditional preoccupation, even obsession, with the morality of particular types of moral acts. Again, this does not imply the validity of another extreme: "Anything goes" between consenting adults who believe that they are not harming one another. It does imply, first, that the nature of the Christian life as a whole is of primary importance, and that moral choices are expressions of it; and, second, that particular actions are not in and of themselves constitutive of one's entire relation to God. The biblical scholar Eugene LaVerdiere comments that, for the early Christian communities that produced the New Testament, sexual attitudes and conduct flowed from the new life of Christians, the gospel internalized, which was "the wellspring of right living as well as the point of departure for ethical reflection."[3] References to sexual morality in the Gospels and Epistles reveal that "sexual ethics is grounded in a strong sense of the Christians' new identity in Christ as well as in their community solidarity."[4]

THE SEXUAL NORM

Although the biblical materials do not yield a code of Christian sexual morality, specified in comprehensive detail, they do provide a normative overview of the meaning of sexuality, as well as some indication of the sorts of acts incompatible with that meaning. Perspectives on sexuality in both Testaments favor the institutionalization of sexuality in heterosexual, monogamous, permanent, and procreative marriage that furthers the cohesiveness and continuity of family, church, and body politic, and that respects and nurtures the affective commitments to which spouses give sexual expression. The biblical literature also provides specific condemnations of deviations from this general norm: *adultery* (Lev. 20:10; Gen. 39:9; Prov. 2:17; Sir. 23:16–21; Exod. 20:14; Deut. 5:18; Mark 7:22; Matt. 5:28; 15:19; 1 Cor. 6:9); *fornication* (Sir. 42:10; Deut. 22:13–21; Lev. 19:29); *porneia* or "sexual immorality" (Mark 7:21; Matt. 15:19; 1 Cor. 5:9–11; 7:2; 2 Cor. 12:21; Gal. 15:19; Eph. 5:3, 5); and *homosexual acts* (Lev. 18:22; 20:13; Rom. 1:27; 1 Cor. 6:9). These prohibited acts are excluded because they are incompatible with the life of faith in the covenant community; but it is the nature of this community and the marks of membership in it that most involve the attention of the biblical authors. Not one of these prohibitions is offered as the result of, or a substitute for, an inclusive meditation on the meaning of human sexuality or a detailed sexual ethics. As the New Testament hermeneutic of the divorce texts demonstrates, even the teachings of Jesus do not necessarily exclude all exceptions, though such exceptions are not specified. The concern ever guiding admonitions, prohibitions, and permissions is to elucidate and enjoin the sort of life characteristic of the people of God.

When the ethicist turns to normative interpretations of biblical materials concerning sexuality, he or she is confronted with now familiar questions: If the canon does favor a certain fundamental norm of human relationships, does that give it unquestioned authority? How is a general norm to be applied in practice? And what is the role of resources beyond the Bible in answering these questions? In the first place, it certainly will be asked whether the authority of the "norm" of heterosexual monogamy differs in any crucial sense from a "norm" such as patriarchy whose decisiveness for Christian faith, practice, and theology is dubious. It is arguable that both monogamy and patriarchy are confirmed by Christian tradition, by empirical studies (e.g., cross-cultural anthropology), and, at least until recently, by most mainstream philosophical anthropologies.

The affirmation of the general norm of monogamy, but not patriarchy, depends in the end on an admittedly circular construal of central Christian images and human insights.[5] The conclusion that monogamy is consistent with what is meant by the normatively "human" and "Christian," but that sexual hierarchy is not, is a "demonstrable" judgment, rather than a "verifiable" one in a logical or empirical sense. The demonstration consists in appeal to a critical norm brought to Scripture with the aid of Christian ethics' complementary sources. The persuasiveness of the norm depends on a reasonable consensus, based both on immediate experience and on normative reflection employing philosophical categories and central Christian images, that human persons are images of God, and by definition are capable of and are most fully human when enjoying goods such as freedom, rationality, sociality, cooperation, commitment, fidelity, and equality. Redeemed humanity, understood with the Christian symbols of cross and resurrection, is repentant for abuses of these goods, is transformed as "new creation," and is dedicated to equality, harmony, and fidelity in the Lord, even when they require self-sacrifice.

In turn, the social and interpersonal meanings of sexual experience are realized most completely when sex is pleasurable, reciprocal, affective, unitive, and procreative. Sexual trivialization, glorification, manipulation, narcissism, and infidelity are not consistent with these themes, but sexual and gender equality are; marriage ideally enhances these goods but sexual hierarchy does not.

It is less clear, however, that the prohibitions that biblical authors derive from the monogamous, heterosexual, and procreative meanings of sexuality unfailingly indicate specific relations and acts that decisively fail to embody those goods that meaningful sexuality is said to realize. We have seen that the Bible itself provides for occasional exceptions or unusual applications whose status as such does not threaten the status of the norm against which they are defined. Marriage in ancient Israel occasionally was polygynous (Gen. 29:21–30; 2 Sam. 5:13–16; 1 Kings 11:1, 3) or was accompanied by concubinage (Gen. 16:1–4; 30:1–13). Levirate marriage (Gen. 38:8; Deut. 25:5–10) augmented the production of heirs. Marriage could be dissolved by divorce at the husband's initiative (Deut. 24:1–4; but cf. Mal. 2:14–16). In the New Testament, divorce of some sort was permitted by Matthew and Paul. On the biblical model, the question of exceptions appears to be an open one. How then shall the viability of proposed exceptions be determined?

USING EMPIRICAL
INFORMATION

The special helpfulness of descriptive, especially empirical, research lies in its ability to illumine the *reality* of situations that the ethicist evaluates. This does not necessarily make empirical studies a uniformly more important ethical source than tradition and philosophy, but in the present historical, socio-cultural context, they offer some of the most provocative evidence and further the critique of other sources upon which Christian ethics has relied more frequently in the past. While these studies bear out the pervasiveness of the institutionalization of sex in marriage and family, they also clarify the circumstances of variance. Certainly not all societies accommodate sex, marriage, and procreation in the same ways, nor do individuals engage in nonprocreative or nonmarital sexual activity for the same reasons, with the same motives, or with the same social and personal consequences.

The contribution that empirical evidence has made to the Christian evaluation of homosexuality is a case in point. The biblical tradition has been associated by and large with negative prohibitions of homosexuality. Recently the empirical sciences have been associated with challenges to biblically supported condemnations of homosexual acts as "unnatural," "ungodly," and "wrong." Since Christians not only come from a faith tradition but are also human beings living in human societies in history, it is necessary to take these challenges seriously. The sciences of anthropology, sociology, psychology, and biology have turned a good deal of attention to and have a good deal to say about the phenomenon of human being as sexual being, including homosexual being. The homosexual orientation and relationship are today understood to differ from what most biblical and traditional authors interpreted simply as willful perversion.[6]

Alfred Kinsey was among the first to establish some reliable instruments for documenting the incidence and variety of homosexual behavior.[7] According to his studies, only 4 percent of males and 2 to 3 percent of females are "exclusively homosexual throughout their lives," but 37 percent of males and 13 percent of females have had a least one significant homosexual experience after adolescence.[8] It also has been estimated that the population of the United States includes two million homosexuals.[9] In 1973, the American Psychiatric Association removed homosexuality from its diagnostic manual of psychiatric disorders.[10] In 1982 the Kinsey Institute also suggested that homosexuality may have a biological basis, and that 10 percent of children appear to lack from a very early age a strong gender conformity and an attraction to the toys and games traditionally favored by their gender.[11] Some researchers have offered evidence that homosexuality may originate in the genetic makeup of the human zygote, and may be related to chromosomal and hormonal anomalies.[12] Whatever its origins, and, in fact, these may very well be diverse, the homosexual orientation and its accompanying life styles can take many forms.[13] These forms occur cross-culturally, although perhaps not universally. And it has been demonstrated by anthropologists[14] and historians[15] that different cultures vary in acceptance, rejection, and even institutionalization of homosexuality. Although most psychiatrists in Western culture do not advocate therapy aimed at changing the sexual orientation of persons who are exclusively homosexual by the Kinsey scale, they do appreciate the importance of assisting the homosexual person to improve self-image, interpersonal relationships, and social adjustment. The evaluative norm for these "improvements" appears to be ability to sustain stable, affective, sexual relationships, particularly with one other person.[16]

What does the increasingly plentiful data about the frequency and etiology of a human sexual phenomenon like homosexuality "prove" about its moral character? Despite the fact that homosexuality remains incompletely understood, we find what appears to be a consensus that most persons discover their sexual orientation as a "given," if an ambiguous and confusing given, rather than choosing it. Furthermore, homosexuality is a variation in human sexual orientation that occurs consistently even though with less frequency than heterosexuality. Although neither consistency nor frequency in and of themselves establish whether a phenomenon of human constitution or behavior is biologically or psychologically healthy or pathological,[17] much less whether it is morally right or wrong, they do have implications for moral judgment. If certain biological or psychological conditions constantly recur in human societies, then the members of those societies have the obligation to enhance human life as far as possible in the midst of those conditions, whether the conditions themselves are desirable or undesirable.

Empirical studies are able to tell us something about the cooperation of male and female physiology in reproduction; about the relative frequency of conception in humans; about the nature and causes of sexual pleasure; about the psychic components of human sexual interaction. They also are able to discriminate between male and female sexual response, both physiological and psychological, and tell us something about the roles that sexual interactions and commitments play in society, culture, and history. But they are not able, by dint of empirically based description alone, to tell us conclusively what place such factors *ought* to have. Beyond the level of the de facto occurrence of certain behaviors or social arrangements, there lie the levels of biological and psychological evaluation, and, finally, of moral evaluation. It is necessary to introduce moral categories in order to move beyond statistical norms, and even beyond norms of "health," which depend to some extent upon *evaluation* of what is observed to occur in "nature." No simple definitions of what is morally "normative," or even what is "healthy," in human sexuality will be available from sheer empirical investigations, even though the latter augment ethical reflection immensely. It must be remembered that even empirical "data" are organized and interpreted with the help of categories that are themselves not wholly "value free." The decisive question for Christian ethics is which "naturally" occurring and even functionally "healthy" facts, states, and relations also represent moral ideals. Empirical evidence can be appropriated meaningfully in Christian ethics only if interpreted in the light of other, complementary sources: Scripture, tradition, and normative, as distinct from descriptive, accounts of the human.

FORMULATING MORAL
CRITERIA

In considering the morality of departures from the central Christian sexual norm of a lasting procreative union of one woman and one man, I suggest two things. First, the Christian community should formulate criteria that define fidelity to the essence of this norm, while allowing variance in the ways it is fulfilled. Some leeway at the level of practice would permit attention to and respect for the responsibility of moral agents in concrete circumstances to realize human and Christian values within special social contexts. Second, it is necessary to contemplate true departures from norms as well as unusual applications of them, though the vast majority of "exceptions" will fall into the latter category. Departures even from the essential meaning of the norm, while they should be rare, are not intolerable if they represent the most morally commendable courses of action concretely available to individuals caught in those tragic or ambiguous situations that agonize the decision maker and vex the analyst. Finally, fixation of attention on the outer limits of applications and departures is not a perspective on sexuality congruent with the biblical one; biblical authors are above all concerned with the shape of the covenant community, and, regarding sexuality, with how relations between the sexes express the authenticity of faith.

It has not been unusual for Christian authors to define the significance of sexuality in terms of two aspects or purposes that are at the heart of the traditional norm of marriage. These are *committed partnership* and *procreation*. In continuity with this line of thought, contemporary authors, with greater appreciation of the affective, interpersonal dimension of sexual commitment and cooperation, speak of "love" and see it on a level equal to that of procreation, not as a secondary value. Pope Paul VI, for instance, speaks of the "unitive" and "procreative" meanings of "the conjugal act," and further defines the former as "true mutual love."[18] The Second Vatican

Council's *Pastoral Constitution on the Church in the Modern World* similarly mentions "mutual self-giving and human procreation in the context of true love."[19] Gathering biblical resources for his discussion of sexual morality, the Protestant theologian Paul Ramsey appeals to God's own creative acts of love in concluding that an act of sexual intercourse has "two goods, or intrinsic ends," which are "its relational or unitive and its procreative purpose."[20]

Building on and interpreting these meanings of sexuality, the essential criteria of Christian sexual responsibility in practice might be formulated as (1) an intentionally permanent commitment of partnership and love; and (2) the willingness of the couple to welcome and nurture as a couple any children that result from their union. If these standards are valid, the Christian could exercise responsible sexuality in certain circumstances in which strict adherence to the norm of procreative, heterosexual monogamy is inappropriate, difficult, or impossible. Examples of application of the central criteria of sexual conduct to situations that fall outside the usual marital standard are remarriage after divorce; committed but premarital ("preceremonial"[21]) sex; the avoidance of conception in conjugal sexual relations; and even the committed homosexual relationship. Expressions of sexuality that are not justifiable according to these criteria are adultery; full sexual relations between partners committed neither to one another nor to possible offspring; and any subtly coercive or openly violent sexual activity, even if it occurs between spouses. It is in the nature of the case, I suspect, that if there are sexual acts that truly violate the norm, but that are morally responsible, they cannot be gathered together under any "rules." Their justifiability would be contingent upon the convergence of circumstances in a moral dilemma that the agent finds insoluble, except at the cost of "sinning bravely," that is, of causing some evil for what is perceived as an *obligatory* good. I am not willing to disallow in principle the possibility of moral conflicts so radical that the agents caught in them cannot be absolved by refraining from the "direct" causation of material evil, by taking as an absolute the principle "Do no harm," or by refusing to decide. Although the moral universe of the ideally "natural" or of the mind of God may be orderly, human moral existence as we know it, live it, and often suffer it, can be impregnable to human efforts to render it coherent.

CONCLUSIONS

Having offered these normative reflections, I hope to conclude in a tone that is irenic, ecumenical, and cautious.[22] Sexual morality is a difficult subject, one that impinges in a most intimate and often painful way on the consciences, identities, anxieties, and hopes of those who address it. In the churches, as in the wider culture, sexuality has been a source of division, exclusion, suffering, and even hatred. Remorse about complicity in this fact and a resolve to remedy it do not necessarily mean that those who have been on different sides of the question will abandon theoretical and practical disagreements, or that efforts to discern better the truths of the matter should be at an end. Various theological and moral perceptions of sexuality still need to be formulated with an appropriate degree of humility as well as honesty. It also needs to be allowed not only that those positions that one regards as untrue may be held sincerely and conscientiously but also that one's own positions, however deeply believed, might be in need of revision.

As the study of New Testament perspectives on morality has made perfectly clear, moral norms and criteria for application do not—in the best of Christian tradition—amount to an abstract, ahistorical, and unchanging code. The *community* itself, and the experience of its members in the Spirit, is the primary reference of moral evaluation, and also the primary basis from which moral discernment proceeds. Says LaVerdiere, "The New Testament thus challenges the church to build genuine communities in which sexual behavior can be recognized as disruptive or constructive of community life."[23] The Christian community is charged to encourage and sustain *processes of recognition* that are true to its own historical experience as covenant people of God. This experience is not utterly new in every age, for the community is still the community of the same Lord and is made up of the same humanity, created, called, and redeemed. But humanity is a creation made to accept its own finitude, and sent forth from the garden wondering about its destiny; the people is a people in progress; and the Lord is the God who shows forth commandments, judgment, and mercy in partial and puzzling signs.

Certainly the foremost historical arrangement that structures and facilitates the contributions of human sexuality, and deflects perversion of its power, is marriage. Through marriage, the partnership of the couple is given social support and is linked to other communal and cultural relationships and lines of order. Through marriage, the individual as spouse, parent, child, or sibling, is linked to the larger communities of family, tribe, race, or nation. But the conditions that allow this relationship to emerge and make it fruitful are not present always and everywhere that human sexuality is present. More important, the realities of sex and marriage and parenthood are as historical as the agents who experience them. The Christian community as a community of moral discernment must continually ask what these realities signify for those who integrate them concretely with faith commitments and secular or nonreligious responsibilities and relationships. The evaluative perspective of the community must comprehend its own experience with its diversity and change as well as its lines of continuity.

How, for instance, shall the charism of celibacy be understood in an age in which the end time (*eschaton*) has receded and it has become dubious that sexual abstinence is a precondition of thoroughgoing religious commitment? How shall marriage be understood in a society whose basic organization no longer depends on kinship, and in a world where unlimited procreation would be an evil not a good? How shall the sexual identity of the single adult be understood in a culture in which marital and familial ties no longer define social identity and roles, in which the assumption that all adults shall wed has become problematic, and in which the expressive, pleasurable, and companionable potentials of sex receive widespread appreciation and even promotion? How shall the homosexual's situation be understood after empirical studies have indicated the relative uncontrollability of sexual orientation, along with the fundamental relation of sexuality to identity and personality? Shifts in sexual milieus do not necessarily mean that Christian ethics needs to be rewritten entirely, but it may require radical reappropriation of the images by which it is informed. Responsibility in sexuality is no more an either/or, black-and-white matter than it is in other moral spheres such as economics, war and peace, or ecology. Exercises of sexuality that fulfill or depart from the norm are not all equally good or equally bad. I have proposed two criteria, commitment and procreative responsibility, that are susceptible of differing realizations, and of realization in varying degrees. This proposal is intended to be dialogic rather than definitive. It should now be clear that the Christian ethicist and every morally serious Christian should be engaged in the critical, communal task of refining criteria of sexual acts and relationships. The horizon against which *all* moral activity is to be evaluated is the communal life as body of Christ in the world.

NOTES

1. The general framework of this final chapter was worked out in "Humanity as Male and Female: The Ethics of Sexuality," a presentation for the 1984 Villanova Theology Institute, included in *Called to Love: Towards a Contemporary Christian Ethic*, ed. Francis A. Eigo (Villanova, Pa.: Theology Institute Publications, 1984); and also is reflected in "Sexual Ethics," an entry I contributed to the *Dictionary of Christian Ethics*, 2d ed., ed. James F. Childress (Philadelphia: Westminster Press, 1984).

2. For development of the idea that procreation is intrinsically related to sex, see my chapter "On the Connection of Sex to Reproduction," in *Sexuality and Medicine*, ed. Earl E. Shelp (Boston and Dordrecht, Neth.: D. Reidel Pub. Co., forthcoming).

3. Eugene LaVerdiere, "The Witness of the New Testament," in *Dimensions of Human Sexuality*, ed. Dennis Doherty (New York: Doubleday & Co., 1979), 25.

4. Ibid., 35. See also Victor Paul Furnish, *The Moral Teaching of Paul: Selected Issues* (Nashville: Abingdon Press, 1979), 22.

5. David H. Kelsey compares a theological position to an Alexander Calder mobile, in which various constituent parts are hung in constantly shifting balance. Theological proposals emerge from the circular relation among uses of Scripture in the common life of the church, the theologian's construal of God's presence, the theologian's use of the Bible as "scripture" for theology, and theology's critique of the church. See *The Uses of Scripture in Recent Theology* (Philadelphia: Fortress Press, 1975), 205–6.

6. Robin Scroggs is particularly helpful in elucidating the socio-cultural contexts of biblical prohibitions of homosexuality (*The New Testament and Homosexuality* (Philadelphia: Fortress Press, 1983).

7. Alfred Kinsey et al., *Sexual Behavior in the Human Male* (Philadelphia: Saunders, 1948); and Alfred Kinsey et al., *Sexual Behavior in the Human Female* (Philadelphia: Saunders, 1953).

8. Kinsey, *Human Male*, 651.

9. Jack Thomas, "Television: A Courageous Look at Growing up Gay" *The Boston Globe* (5 January, 1983): 57.

10. Charles N. Socarides, M.D., "Homosexuality Is Not Just an Alternative Life Style," in *Male and Female: Christian Approaches to Sexuality*, ed. Ruth Tiffany Barnhouse and Urban T. Holmes III (New York: Seabury Press, 1976), 149.

11. Thomas, "Growing Up Gay," 57.

12. James A. Monteleone, M.D., "The Physiological Aspects of Sex," in *Human Sexuality and Personhood: Proceedings of the Workshop for the Hierarchies of the United States and Canada Sponsored by the Pope John Center through a Grant from the Knights of Columbus* (St. Louis: Pope John Center, 1981), 71–85.

13. Alan P. Bell and Martin S. Weinberg, *Homosexualities: A Study of Diversity among Men and Women* (New York: Simon and Schuster, 1978).

14. Margaret Farley, "Sexual Ethics," in *Encyclopedia of Bioethics*, ed. Warren T. Reich (New York: Free Press, 1978), 1583; Clellan S. Ford and Frank A. Beach, *Patterns of Sexual Behavior* (New York: Harper & Brothers, 1951), 130 (cited by Farley); Harriet Whitehead, "The Bow and the Burden Strap: A New Look at Institutionalized Homosexuality in Native North America," *Sexual Meanings* (New York: Cambridge Univ. Press, 1981), 80–115.

15. John Boswell, *Christianity, Social Tolerance, and Homosexuality: Gay People in Western Europe from the Beginning of the Christian Era to the Fourteenth Century* (Chicago: Univ. of Chicago Press, 1980).

16. Bell and Weinberg, *Homosexualities*, 220.

17. The content of the norm "health" is not as self-evident as it might at first appear. One frequently proposed and reasonable definition of biological and psychological health is "the successful functioning of an organism in its environment." This definition lends credence to the proposal that the active homosexual who is personally and socially well-adjusted is also sexually "healthy." However, at second sight, we discover that there is in this definition a certain circularity. The health of a sexual orientation is contingent upon "successful function"; but "success" and even "function" are evaluative concepts that return us to the unavoidable question of what we consider to be adequate or normative human sexual functioning, and whether or not the directing of one's genital sexuality to members of the same sex fulfills that definition, even if one's sexual orientation does not impinge detrimentally upon one's ability to perform other social roles. An *evaluative* component, then, is unavoidable, even in ostensibly "empirical" notions of health and sickness. It is no less problematic when the agenda behind the definition of "health" is the justification of homosexuality, than when it is its denigration by inclusion in a list of psychiatric disorders.

18. Pope Paul VI, *Humanae Vitae: Encyclical Letter on the Regulation of Birth* (Washington D.C.: United States Catholic Conference, 1968), no. 12.

19. *Pastoral Constitution on the Church in the Modern World*, in Walter M. Abbott, S.J., ed., *The Documents of Vatican II* (New York: American Press, 1966), no. 51.

20. Paul Ramsey, *One Flesh: A Christian View of Sex Within, Outside, and Before Marriage* (Nottingham, Eng.: Grove Books, 1975), 4. (The substance of this booklet originally appeared in the *Journal of Religion* 45/2 [1975]: 100–18.)

21. Cf. Ramsey, *One Flesh*, 17–18; C. Jaime Snoek, "Marriage and the Institutionalization of Sexual Relations," in *The Future of Marriage as Institution*, ed. Franz Böckle (New York: Herder & Herder, 1970), 111–22.

22. Without doubt, other Christian authors will have disagreements with my conclusions, and their arguments will not be without merit. One sensitive and different analysis of sexuality is offered by James B. Nelson, in *Between Two Gardens: Reflections on Sexuality and Religious Experience* (New York: Pilgrim Press, 1983). Nelson advances the discussion of "sexual theology" that places genital sexuality in a more complete context. He criticizes the Christian heritage for defining sexuality in terms of two life styles only: celibacy and heterosexual marriage. Nelson argues that a more positive appreciation of sex will inform a more flexible view of those contexts in which sexual expression is commendable.

23. LaVerdiere, "Witness of the New Testament," 36.

SELECT BIBLIOGRAPHY

A.
BIBLICAL
HERMENEUTICS

Barr, James. *Holy Scripture: Canon, Authority, Criticism*. Philadelphia: Westminster Press, 1983.

Birch, Bruce C. "Biblical Hermeneutics in Recent Discussion: Old Testament." *Religious Studies Review* 10 (January 1984): 1–7.

Braaten, Carl E., and Roy A. Harrisville, eds. *The Historical Jesus and the Kerygmatic Christ*. Nashville: Abingdon Press, 1964.

Brown, Raymond E. *The Critical Meaning of the Bible*. New York: Paulist Press, 1981.

Childs, Brevard. *Introduction to the Old Testament as Scripture*. Philadelphia: Fortress Press, 1979.

Dunn, James D. G. *Unity and Diversity in the New Testament: An Inquiry into the Character of Earliest Christianity*. Philadelphia: Westminster Press, 1977.

Greenspahn, Frederick E., ed. *Scripture in the Jewish and Christian Traditions: Authority, Interpretation, Relevance*. Nashville: Abingdon Press, 1982.

Hanson, Paul D. *The Diversity of Scripture: A Theological Interpretation*. Philadelphia: Fortress Press, 1982.

Harrington, Daniel J. "Biblical Hermeneutics in Recent Discussion: New Testament." *Religious Studies Review* 10 (January 1984): 7–10.

Harvey, Van A. *The Historian and the Believer*. New York: Macmillan Co. 1966.

Keck, Leander E. *A Future for the Historical Jesus: The Place of Jesus in Preaching and Theology*. Philadelphia: Fortress Press, 1980.

Kelsey, David H. *The Uses of Scripture in Recent Theology*. Philadelphia: Fortress Press, 1975.

Perrin, Norman. *Rediscovering the Teaching of Jesus.* New York: Harper & Row, 1967.

Ricoeur, Paul. *Essays on Biblical Interpretation.* Philadelphia: Fortress Press, 1980.

Sanders, Jack. "Hermeneutics." In *The Jerome Biblical Commentary*, edited by Raymond E. Brown, Joseph Fitzmyer, Roland E. Murphy, 605–23. Englewood Cliffs, N.J.: Prentice-Hall, 1968.

Schneiders, Sandra M. "From Exegesis to Hermeneutics: The Problem of the Contemporary Meaning of Scripture." *Horizons* 8 (Spring 1981): 23–39.

Schüssler Fiorenza, Elisabeth. "Contemporary Biblical Scholarship: Its Roots, Present Understandings, and Future Directions." In *Modern Biblical Scholarship: Its Impact on Theology and Proclamation*, edited by Francis A. Eigo, O.S.A., 1–36. Villanova, Pa.: Villanova Univ. Press, 1984.

B.
THE BIBLE AND
ETHICS

Birch, Bruce C. and Larry L. Rasmussen. *Bible and Ethics in the Christian Life.* Minneapolis: Augsburg Pub. House, 1976.

Daly, Robert J. *Christian Biblical Ethics: From Biblical Revelation to Contemporary Christian Praxis.* New York: Paulist Press, 1984.

Furnish, Victor Paul. *The Moral Teaching of Paul: Selected Issues.* Nashville: Abingdon Press, 1979.

———. *Theology and Ethics in Paul.* Nashville: Abingdon Press, 1968.

Gustafson, James M. "The Place of Scripture in Christian Ethics: A Methodological Study." In *Theology and Christian Ethics.* New York: Pilgrim Press, 1974.

Houlden, J. L. *Ethics and the New Testament.* New York and London: Oxford Univ. Press, 1977.

Ogletree, Thomas. *The Use of the Bible in Christian Ethics.* Philadelphia: Fortress Press, 1983.

Perkins, Pheme. *Love Commands in the New Testament.* New York: Paulist Press, 1982.

———. "Paul and Ethics." *Interpretation* 38 (July 1984): 268–80.

———. *Ministering in the Pauline Churches.* New York: Paulist Press, 1982.

———. "New Testament Ethics: Questions and Contexts." *Religious Studies Review* 10 (October 1984): 321–27.

Sanders, Jack T. *Ethics in the New Testament.* Philadelphia: Fortress Press, 1975.

Swartly, Willard M. *Slavery, Sabbath, War and Women: Case Issues in Biblical Interpretation.* Scottdale, Pa.: Herald Press, 1983.

Verhey, Allen. "The Use of Scripture in Ethics." *Religious Studies Review* 4 (January 1978): 28–39.

————. *The Great Reversal: Ethics and the New Testament.* Grand Rapids: Wm. B. Eerdmans, 1984.

C.
THE BIBLE AND
THE SEXES

Achtemeier, Elizabeth. *The Committed Marriage.* Philadelphia: Westminster Press, 1978.

Bird, Phyllis A. "'Male and Female He Created Them': Gen. 1:27b in the Context of the Priestly Account of Creation." *Harvard Theological Review* 74/2 (1981): 129–59.

Donahue, John R. "Divorce: New Testament Perspectives." *The Month* 14 (April 1981): 113–120.

Gerstenberger, E. S. and W. Schrage. *Women and Man.* Nashville: Abingdon Press, 1981.

Jensen, Joseph. "Human Sexuality in the Scriptures." In *Human Sexuality and Personhood: Proceedings of the Workshop for the Hierarchies of the United States and Canada Sponsored by the Pope John Center through a Grant from the Knights of Columbus.* St. Louis: Pope John Center, 1981.

Jewett, Paul K. *Man as Male and Female.* Grand Rapids: Wm. B. Eerdmans, 1975.

Kysar, Myrna and Robert Kysar. *The Asundered: Biblical Teaching on Divorce and Remarriage.* Atlanta: John Knox Press, 1978.

Schüssler Fiorenza, Elisabeth. *In Memory of Her: A Feminist Theological Reconstruction of Christian Origins.* New York: Crossroad, 1983.

Scroggs, Robin. *The New Testament and Homosexuality.* Philadelphia: Fortress Press, 1983.

Stendahl, Krister. *The Bible and the Role of Women: A Case Study in Hermeneutics.* Philadelphia: Fortress Press, 1966.

Tetlow, Elisabeth M. *Women and Ministry in the New Testament.* New York: Paulist Press, 1980.

Trible, Phyllis. *God and the Rhetoric of Sexuality.* Philadelphia: Fortress Press, 1978.

D.
DESCRIPTIVE AND
EMPIRICAL STUDIES OF GENDER ROLES
AND HOMOSEXUALITY

Bell, Alan P. and Martin S. Weinberg. *Homosexualities: A Study of Diversity among Men and Women*. New York: Simon and Schuster, 1978.

Boswell, John. *Christianity, Social Tolerance, and Homosexuality: Gay People in Western Europe from the Beginning of the Christian Era to the Fourteenth Century*. Chicago: Univ. of Chicago Press, 1980.

Konner, Melvin. *The Tangled Wing: Biological Constraints on the Human Spirit*. New York: Harper & Row, 1983.

Maccoby, Eleanor and Carol Jacklin. *The Psychology of Sex Differences*. Stanford, Calif.: Stanford Univ. Press, 1974.

Ortner, Sherry B. and Harriet Whitehead, eds. *Sexual Meanings: The Cultural Construction of Gender and Sexuality*. New York: Cambridge Univ. Press, 1981.

Pleck, Joseph. *The Myth of Masculinity*. Cambridge, Mass.: M.I.T. Press, 1981.

Rosaldo, Michelle Z. "The Use and Abuse of Anthropology." *Signs* (Spring 1980): 389–417.

Rosaldo, Michelle Zimbalist and Louise Lamphere, eds. *Women, Culture and Society*. Stanford, Calif.: Stanford Univ. Press, 1974.

Sanday, Peggy Reeves. *Female Power and Male Dominance: On the Origins of Sexual Inequality*. New York: Cambridge Univ. Press, 1981.

E.
PHILOSOPHICAL
PERSPECTIVES ON HUMANITY
AND SEXUALITY

Baker, Robert and Frederick Elliston, eds. *Philosophy and Sex*. Buffalo: Prometheus Books, 1975.

Jeanniere, Abel. *The Anthropology of Sex*. New York: Harper & Row, 1967.

Midgley, Mary. *Beast and Man*. Ithaca, N.Y.: Cornell Univ. Press, 1978.

F.
CHRISTIAN SEXUAL
ETHICS

For primary works of Aquinas and Luther, consult notes, chaps. 6 and 7.

Avvento, Gennaro P. *Sexuality: A Christian View*. Mystic, Conn.: Twenty-Third Publications, 1982.

Barnhouse, Ruth Tiffany and Urban T. Holmes III, eds. *Male and Female: Christian Approaches to Sexuality.* New York: Seabury Press, 1976.

Børreson, Kari Elisabeth. *Subordination and Equivalence: The Nature and Role of Women in Augustine and Thomas Aquinas.* Washington, D.C.: Univ. Press of America, 1981.

Doherty, Dennis, ed. *Dimensions of Human Sexuality.* New York: Doubleday & Co., 1979.

Farley, Margaret. "Sexual Ethics." In *Encyclopedia of Bioethics*, edited by Warren T. Reich. New York: Free Press, 1978.

Fuchs, Eric. *Sexual Desire and Love: Origins and History of the Christian Ethic of Sexuality and Marriage.* New York: Seabury Press, 1983.

Goergen, Donald. *The Sexual Celibate.* New York: Seabury Press, 1975.

Guindon, Andre. *The Sexual Language: An Essay in Moral Theology.* Ottawa: Univ. of Ottawa Press, 1976.

Gustafson, James M. "Nature, Sin, and Covenant: Three Bases for Sexual Ethics." *Perspectives in Biology and Medicine* 24 (Spring 1981): 493–97.

Huddleston, Mary Anne, ed. *Celibate Loving: Encounter in Three Dimensions.* New York: Paulist Press, 1984.

Kasper, Walter. *Theology of Christian Marriage.* New York: Crossroad, 1981.

Keane, Philip S. *Sexual Morality: A Catholic Perspective.* New York: Paulist Press, 1977.

Kelly, David F. "Sexuality and Concupiscence in Augustine." In *The Annual of the Society of Christian Ethics: 1983*, edited by Larry L. Rasmussen. Distributed by the Council on the Study of Religion, Wilfrid Laurier University, Waterloo, Ontario, 1983.

Kosnick, Anthony et al. *Human Sexuality: New Directions in American Catholic Thought.* New York: Paulist Press, 1977.

Mackin, Theodore. *What is Marriage?* New York: Paulist Press, 1983.

————. *Divorce and Remarriage.* New York/Ramsey, N.J.: Paulist Press, 1984.

Mehl, Roger. *Society and Love: Ethical Problems of Family Life.* Philadelphia: Westminster Press, 1964.

Nelson, James B. *Between Two Gardens: Reflections on Sexuality and Religious Experience.* New York: Pilgrim Press, 1983.

————. *Embodiment: An Approach to Sexuality and Christian Theology.* Minneapolis: Augsburg Pub. House, 1978.

Ramsey, Paul. *One Flesh: A Christian View of Sex Within, Outside, and Before Marriage.* Nottingham, Eng.: Grove Books, 1975.

SUBJECT INDEX

Accounts of the human:
  descriptive: 1, 5–6, 9–10, 37–38,
    52, 60, 72, 85–89, 144, 145–48;
    in Aquinas, 107–10, 113, 118–
    19; in Luther, 9–10, 128–30,
    136
  normative: 1, 5–6, 9–10, 13, 38,
    52, 56, 60, 72, 85–89, 144, 147;
    in Aquinas, 9–10, 107–9; in
    Luther, 9–10, 125–126
Adultery, 18, 19, 64, 74, 143, 149;
  in Aquinas, 115; in Luther, 131,
  137
Anthropology: cross-cultural, 7, 86,
  92–96, 103–4, 142, 144, 145;
  philosophical, 5–6, 9, 54, 85, 87,
  109, 115–16

Baruch, Book of, 40
Biblical interpretation. *See*
  Hermeneutics, biblical
Birth control, 108, 120, 149, 153

Canon: biblical, 8, 15–44, 62, 71–
  72, 84, 115, 143; definition of, 39
Canon within the canon, 20–21, 25,
  42
Celibacy, 18, 59, 60, 61, 66, 67, 68,
  76, 78, 139, 140, 154; in Aquinas,
  105, 107, 114, 115–16, 119, 122;
  in Luther, 123, 124, 130–31, 133,
  151
Colossians, Letter to, 59, 64

Common good (communal good), 8,
  53, 60, 67–68, 72–73, 139, 142–
  43, 150, 152
Concubinage, 115, 145
Contraception. *See* Birth control
Corinthians, First Letter to, 19, 27,
  45, 59, 61, 62–72, 73–77, 79, 80,
  81, 143; in Aquinas, 115, 117; in
  Luther, 125, 131, 132, 134
Corinthians, Second Letter to, 143

Desire: sexual, 2–4, 12, 55, 63, 140;
  in Aquinas, 106, 113, 114; in
  Luther, 124, 126, 134. *See also*
  Experience, sexual; Pleasure,
  sexual
Deuteronomy, Book of, 143, 145
Divorce: in Aquinas, 115; in
  Luther, 131–32, 137; New
  Testament texts on, 9, 12, 60, 61,
  64, 73–77, 81, 143

Ecclesiasticus, Book of (Sirach), 39,
  143
Ephesians, Letter to, 61, 66, 143; in
  Aquinas, 114, 117
Equality of the sexes, 10, 26, 27–
  29, 35–36, 42, 45, 46, 47–48, 50,
  53, 56, 63, 70–72, 79, 83–104,
  144; in Aquinas, 111–12; in
  Luther 126. *See also* Hierarchy of
  the sexes; Patriarchy

161

AUTHOR INDEX